Y0-BDS-852

Lit. for Reason

Lit. as Poetry

Doyle/Thoreau

LIT. FOR COMPOSITION

Parables, Essays, Stories & Poems

Essay 4

① Final Draft
② Work cited
③ Planning, Drafting, outlining
④ Peer Review
⑤ 5 Avg Sentences

Bedford/St. Martin's   BOSTON ◆ NEW YORK

Copyright © 2012 by Bedford/St. Martin's

All rights reserved. No part of this book may be reproduced, stored in a retrieval system, or transmitted in any form or by any means, electronic, mechanical, photocopying, recording, or otherwise, except as may be expressly permitted by the applicable copyright statutes or in writing by the Publisher.

Manufactured in the United States of America.

For information, write: Bedford/St. Martin's, 75 Arlington Street, Boston, MA 02116 (617-399-4000)

Contents

Lit. for Experience

Lit. for Character

CONTENTS

Lit. for Values

Lit. for Experience

Reading Processes

What's so special about college reading? Don't you pick up the book, start on the first page, and keep going, just as you have ever since you met *The Cat in the Hat*? Reading from beginning to end works especially well when you are eager to find out what happens next, as in a thriller, or what to do next, as in a cookbook. On the other hand, much of what you read in college—textbooks, scholarly articles, research reports, your peers' papers—is complicated and challenging. Dense material like this often requires closer reading and deeper thinking—in short, a process for reading critically.

Reading critically is a useful skill. For assignments in this course alone, you probably will need to evaluate the strengths and weaknesses of essays by professionals and students. If you research any topic, you will need to figure out what your sources say, whether they are reliable, and how you might use their information. Critical reading is important in other courses too. For example, you might analyze a sociology report on violent children for its assumptions and implications as well as the soundness of its argument. When your writing relies on critical reading, you generally need to explain what is going on in the reading material and then go further, making your own point based on what you have read.

A PROCESS OF CRITICAL READING

Reading critically means approaching whatever you read in an active, questioning manner. This essential college-level skill changes reading from a spectator sport to a contact sport. You no longer sit in the stands, watching figure skaters glide by. Instead, you charge right into a rough-and-tumble hockey game, gripping your stick and watching out for your teeth.

X. J. Kennedy, Dorothy M. Kennedy, and Marcia F. Muth, *Writing and Revising: A Portable Guide*, pages 11–21. Copyright © 2007 by Bedford/St. Martin's.

2

Critical reading, like critical thinking, is not an isolated activity. It is a continuum of strategies that thoughtful people use every day to grapple with new information, to integrate it with existing knowledge, and to apply it to problems in daily life and in academic courses. Many readers use similar strategies:

- They get ready to do their reading.
- They respond as they read.
- They read on literal and analytical levels.

■ **ACTIVITY: Describing Your Own Reading Process**

How do you read a magazine, newspaper, or popular novel? What are your goals when you do this kind of reading? What's different about reading the material assigned in college? What techniques do you use for reading assignments? Which of your strategies might help your classmates, especially in classes with a lot of reading? How might you read more effectively?

Preparing to Read

College reading is active reading. Before you read, think ahead about how to approach the reading process, how to make the most of the time you spend reading.

Thinking about Your Purpose. Naturally, your overall goal for doing most college reading is to succeed in your courses. When you begin to read, ask questions like these about your immediate purpose:

- What are you reading?
- Why are you reading?
- What do you want to do with the reading?
- What does your instructor expect you to learn from the reading?
- Do you need to memorize details, find main points, or connect ideas?
- How does this reading build on, add to, contrast with, or otherwise relate to other reading assignments in the course?

Planning Your Follow-up. When you are assigned a specific essay, chapter, or article or are required to choose a reading about a certain topic, ask yourself what your instructor probably expects to follow the reading:

- Do you need to be ready to discuss the reading during class?
- Will you need to mention it or analyze it during an examination?
- Will you need to write about it or its topic?
- Do you need to find its main points? Sum it up? Compare it? Question it? Discuss its strengths and weaknesses? Draw useful details from it?

Skimming the Text. Before you actively read a text, begin by skimming it, quickly reading only enough to introduce yourself to its content and organization. If the reading has a table of contents or subheadings, read those first to figure out what the material covers and how it is organized. Read the first paragraph and then the first (or first and last) sentence of each paragraph that follows. If the material has any illustrations or diagrams, read the captions.

Responding to Reading

Encourage yourself to read energetically by monitoring both what you read and how you respond to it.

Reading Deeply. The books and articles assigned in college often require more concentration from you as a reader than simpler readings do. Use the following questions to help you understand the complexities below the surface of a reading:

- Are difficult or technical terms defined in specific ways? How might you highlight, list, or record those terms so that you can master them?
- How might you record or recall the details in the reading? How might you track or diagram interrelated ideas to grasp the connections?
- How does word choice, tone, or style alert you to the complex purpose of a reading that is layered or indirect rather than straightforward?
- How might you trace the progression of ideas in the reading? Where do you spot headings, previews of what's coming up, summaries of what's gone before, transitions, and other clues to the reading's organization?
- Does the reading include figurative or descriptive language, allusions to other works, or recurring themes? How do these elements enrich the reading?

Keeping a Reading Journal. A reading journal helps you read actively and build a reservoir of ideas for follow-up writing. You can use a special notebook or computer file to address questions like these:

- What is the subject of the reading? What is the writer's stand?
- What does the writer take for granted? What assumptions does he or she begin with? Where are these assumptions stated or suggested?
- What evidence supports the writer's main points?
- Do you agree with what the writer is saying? Do his or her ideas clash with your ideas or call into question something you take for granted?
- Has the writer taken account of other views, opinions, or interpretations of evidence?
- What conclusions can you draw from the reading?
- Has the reading opened your eyes to new ways of viewing the subject?

Annotating the Text. Writing notes on the page (or on a photocopy if the material is not your own) is a useful way to trace the author's points and to respond to them with questions or comments. You can underline key points, mark checks and stars by ideas when you agree or disagree, and jot questions in the margins. (A Critical Reading Checklist appears later in this chapter.) When one student investigated the history of women's professional sports, she annotated a key passage from an article called "Why Men Fear Women's Teams" by Kate Rounds from the January–February 1991 issue of *Ms.*

different case from individual sports

By contrast, women's professional (team) sports have failed spectacularly. Since the mid-seventies, every professional league — softball, basketball, and volleyball — has gone belly-up. In 1981, after a four-year struggle, the Women's Basketball League (WBL), backed by sports promoter Bill Byrne, folded. The league was drawing fans in a number of cities, but the sponsors weren't there, TV wasn't there, and nobody seemed to miss the spectacle of a few good women fighting for a basketball. Or a (volleyball,) for that matter. Despite the success of (bikini) volleyball, an organization called MLV (Major League Volleyball) bit the dust in March of 1989 after nearly three years of

key point

✓

bitter tone

1st example backs up point

✓

Something I know about!

What women's teams have gotten these?

Why does she call it this?

2nd example

5

struggling for sponsorship, fan support, and television exposure.

She's suspicious of men

[As with pro basketball, there was a man behind women's professional volleyball,] real estate investor Robert (Bat) Batinovich. Batinovich admits that, unlike court volleyball,

oh, great

beach volleyball has a lot of "visual T&A mixed into it."

seems like these are only two options

What court volleyball does have, according to former

credential

MLV executive director Lindy Vivas, is strong women athletes. Vivas is assistant volleyball coach at San Jose State University.

Why do guys always think we're weak and prissy?

"The United States in general," she says, "has problems dealing with women athletes and strong, aggressive females. The perception is you have to be more aggressive in team sports than in golf and tennis, which aren't contact sports. Women athletes are looked at as masculine and get the stigma of being gay."

good quote

This student's annotations helped her deepen her reading of the article and generate ideas for her writing.

■ **ACTIVITY: Annotating a Passage**

Annotate the following passage from the middle of Ellen Goodman's essay "Kids, Divorce, and the Myth" from the *Boston Globe Online* (September 28, 2000).

Not that long ago, when the divorce statistics first began to rise, many Americans comforted themselves with the belief that parents and children shared the same perspective. A child in an unhappy home would surely know it, surely suffer from it. What was right for parents—including divorce—was right for children.

But today that seems like a soothing or perhaps self-serving myth.

One of the myth-busters is Judith Wallerstein, who has been studying the children of divorce for over twenty-five years. Her latest book about *The Unexpected Legacy of Divorce* is written about and for the offspring of splintered families, children who carry the family rupture into their adulthood.

This psychologist has followed 131 children of 80 California families, a small and not-so-random sample of the one million children whose parents divorce each year. Today a quarter of all adults under forty-four come from divorced homes, and Wallerstein takes a handful of these

Attitude of author

Stat

children to show in rich detail the way divorce was and remains a life-transforming event.

Her book echoes with the laments of their tribe. These are adults who *another opinion* spent childhood negotiating between two parents and two homes. Some were emotionally abandoned, others were subject to the crazy postdivorce years. Some still wait for disaster, and others are stronger for the struggle.

But as the elder to their tribe, Wallerstein makes one central and challenging point: "The myth that if the parents have a poor marriage the children are going to be unhappy is not true." *her conclusion not scientific*

A SPOTLIGHT ON READING LEVELS

Educational expert Benjamin Bloom identified six levels of cognitive activity: knowledge, comprehension, application, analysis, synthesis, and evaluation.[1] Each level acts as a foundation for the next. Each also becomes more complex and demands higher thinking skills than the previous one. (See Fig. 1.) Experienced readers, however, may jump among these levels, gathering information and insight as they occur.

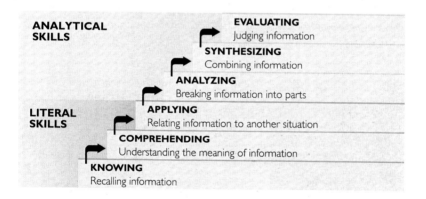

Figure 1. **Using Literal and Analytical Reading Skills.**
SOURCE: The information in this figure is adapted from Benjamin S. Bloom et al., *Taxonomy of Educational Objectives, Handbook 1: Cognitive Domain* (New York: McKay, 1956).

---

[1]Benjamin S. Bloom et al., *Taxonomy of Educational Objectives, Handbook 1: Cognitive Domain.* Copyright © 1956 by David McKay, Inc.

7

The first three levels are literal skills. When you show that you know a fact, comprehend its meaning, and can apply it to a new situation, you demonstrate your mastery over building blocks of thought. The last three levels—analysis, synthesis, and evaluation—are critical skills. These skills take you beyond the literal level: you break apart the building blocks to see what makes them work, recombine them in new and useful ways, and judge their worth or significance. To read critically, you must engage with a piece on both literal and analytical levels.

Reading on Literal Levels

As you first tackle an unfamiliar reading, you may struggle simply to discover what—exactly—it presents to readers. When you read literally, you decode the words in the passage, figure out the meaning, and connect the information to what you already know. For example, suppose you read in your history book a passage about Franklin Delano Roosevelt (FDR), the only American president elected to four consecutive terms of office.

Becoming Aware of the Information. Once you read the passage, even if you have little background in American history, you know and can recall the information it presents about FDR and his four terms in office.

Comprehending the Information. To comprehend the information, you need to know that a term for a U.S. president is four years and that *consecutive* means "continuous." Thus, FDR was elected to serve for sixteen years.

Applying the Information. To apply this knowledge, you think of other presidents—George Washington, who served two terms; Grover Cleveland, who served two terms but not consecutively; Jimmy Carter, who served one term; and Bill Clinton, who served two terms. Then you realize that being elected to four terms is unusual. In fact, the Twenty-Second Amendment to the Constitution, ratified in 1951, now limits a president to two terms.

Reading on Analytical Levels

After mastering a passage on the literal levels, you need to read on the analytical levels, probing the meaning beneath the surface. First, you analyze the information, considering its parts and implications from various angles. Then you gather related material and synthesize all of it, combining it to achieve new insights. Finally, you evaluate the significance of the information.

Analyzing the Information. To return to FDR's four terms as president, you can ask questions to scrutinize this information from various angles, selecting a principle that suits your purpose to break the information into its components or parts. For example, you might analyze FDR's tenure in office in relation to the political longevity of other presidents. Why has FDR been the only president elected to serve four terms? What circumstances during his terms contributed to three reelections? How is FDR different from other presidents?

Synthesizing the Information. To answer your questions, you may have to read more or review material you have read in the past. Then you begin synthesizing—combining information, pulling together the facts and opinions, identifying the evidence accepted by all or most sources, examining any controversial evidence, and drawing whatever conclusions reliable evidence seems to support. For example, it would be logical to conclude that the special circumstances of the Great Depression and World War II contributed to FDR's four terms. On the other hand, it would not be logical to conclude that Americans reelected FDR out of pity because he was a victim of polio.

Evaluating the Information. Finally, you evaluate your new knowledge to determine its significance, both to your understanding of Depression-era politics and to your assessment of your history book's approach. For instance, you might ask yourself why the book's author has chosen to make this point. How does it affect the rest of the discussion? Does this author seem reliable? And you may also have formed your own opinion about FDR's reelections, perhaps concluding that FDR's four-term presidency is understandable in light of the events of the 1930s and 1940s, that the author has mentioned this fact to highlight the unique political atmosphere of that era, and that, in your opinion, it is evidence neither for nor against FDR's excellence as a president.

■ ACTIVITY: Reading Analytically

Think back to something you have read recently that helped you make a decision, perhaps a newspaper or magazine article, an electronic posting, or a college brochure. How did you analyze what you read, breaking the information into parts? How did you synthesize it, combining it with what you already knew? How did you evaluate it, judging its contribution to your decision making?

9

GENERATING IDEAS FROM READING

Like flints that strike each other and cause sparks, writers and readers provoke one another. For example, when your class discusses an essay, you may be surprised by the range of insights your classmates report. If you missed some of their insights during your reading, remember that they may be equally surprised by what you see.

Often you look to other writers—in books or articles—to suggest a topic, provide information about it, or help you explain it or back it up with evidence. You may read because you want to understand ideas, test them, or debate with the writer, but reading is a dynamic process. You may find that it changes your ideas instead of supporting them. Here are suggestions for unlocking the potential hidden in a good text.

Looking for Meaty Pieces. Stimulate your thinking about current topics that intrigue you by browsing through essay collections or magazines in the library or online. Try *The Atlantic, Harper's, The New Republic, Commentary,* or a special-interest magazine like *Architectural Digest* or *Scientific American.* Check the editorials and op-ed columns in your local newspaper, the *New York Times,* or the *Wall Street Journal.* Also search the Internet on interesting subjects that challenge you to think seriously (for example, film classics or the effects of poverty on children). Look for articles that are meaty, not superficial, and that are written to inform and convince, not to entertain or amuse.

Logging Your Reading. For several days keep a log of the articles that you find. Record the author, title, and source for each promising piece so that you can easily find it again. Briefly note the subject and point of view in order to identify a range of possibilities.

Recalling Something You Have Already Read. What have you read lately that started you thinking? Return to a recent reading—a chapter in a humanities textbook, an article assigned in a sociology course, a research study for a biology course.

Capturing Complex Ideas. When you find a challenging reading, do you sometimes feel too overwhelmed to develop ideas from it? If so, read it slowly and carefully. Then consider two common methods of recording and integrating ideas from sources into papers. First, try *paraphrasing,* restating the author's ideas fully but in your own words. Then try *summarizing,* reducing the author's main point to essentials. Accurately restating what a reading says can help you grasp its ideas, especially on literal levels. Once you understand what it says, you are better equipped to agree with, disagree with, or question its points.

Reading Critically. Read first literally and then analytically. Instead of just soaking up what the reading says, engage in a dialogue or conversation with the writer. Criticize. Wonder. Argue back. Demand convincing evidence. Use the following checklist to get you started as a critical reader.

CRITICAL READING CHECKLIST

- ☐ What problems and issues does the author raise?
- ☐ What is the author's purpose? Is it to explain or inform? To persuade? To amuse? In addition to this overall purpose, is the author trying to accomplish some other agenda?
- ☐ How does the author appeal to readers? Where do you agree, and where do you disagree? Where do you want to say "Yeah, right!" or "I don't think so!"?
- ☐ How does this piece relate to your own experiences or thoughts? Have you encountered anything similar? Does the topic or approach intrigue you?
- ☐ Are there any important words or ideas that you don't understand? If so, do you need to reread or turn to a dictionary or reference book?
- ☐ What is the author's point of view? What does the author assume or take for granted? Where does the author reveal these assumptions? Do they make the selection seem weak or biased?
- ☐ Which statements are facts that can be verified by observation, firsthand testimony, or research? Which are opinions? Does one or the other dominate the piece?
- ☐ Is the writer's evidence accurate, relevant, and sufficient? Do you find it persuasive?

Analyzing Writing Strategies. Reading widely and deeply can reveal not only what others say but also how they say it and how they shape such key features as the introduction, thesis statement or main idea, major points, and supporting evidence. Ask questions like those in the following Writing Strategies Checklist to help you identify writing strategies.

WRITING STRATEGIES CHECKLIST

☐ How does the author introduce the reading? In what ways does the author try to engage readers?

☐ Where does the author state or imply the main idea or thesis?

☐ How is the text organized? What are the main points used to develop the thesis? What does the selection of these points suggest about the author's approach?

☐ How does the author supply support—facts, data, statistics, expert opinions, personal experiences, observations, explanations, examples, or other information?

☐ How does the author connect or emphasize ideas for readers?

☐ How does the author conclude the reading?

☐ What is the author's tone? How do the words and examples reveal the author's attitude, biases, or assumptions?

Writing Processes

You are already a writer with long experience. In school you have taken notes, written book reports and term papers, answered exam questions, perhaps kept a journal. You've recorded minutes in community meetings and composed memos on the job. You've e-mailed friends, made shopping lists, maybe even tried your hand at writing songs or poetry. All this experience is about to pay off.

Unlike parachute jumping, writing in college is something you can go ahead and try without first learning all there is to know. In truth, nothing anyone can tell you will help as much as learning by doing. In this book our purpose is to help you write better, deeper, clearer, and more satisfying papers than you have ever written before. We encourage you to do so by diving into writing—experimenting, practicing, and building confidence as you expand your writing strategies.

WRITING, READING, AND CRITICAL THINKING

In college you will perform challenging tasks that enlarge what you already know about writing. In fact, you can view each writing task as a problem to solve, often through careful reading and objective thinking. You will need to read—and write—actively, engaging with the ideas of others. At the same time, you will need to think critically, analyzing and judging those ideas. To help you assess your own achievement, you will use criteria—models, conventions, principles, standards. As you write and rewrite, you can evaluate what you are doing by asking specific questions:

 • Have you considered your audience?
• Have you achieved your purpose?

X. J. Kennedy, Dorothy M. Kennedy, and Marcia F. Muth, *Writing and Revising: A Portable Guide*, pages 1–10. Copyright © 2007 by Bedford/St. Martin's.

• Have you made your point clear by stating it as a thesis or by unmistakably implying it?

 • Have you supported your point with enough reliable evidence to persuade your readers?

 • Have you arranged your ideas logically so that each follows from, supports, or adds to the one before it?

 • Have you made the connections among ideas clear to your readers?

 • Have you established an appropriate tone?

In large measure, learning to write well is learning what questions to ask as you write.

A PROCESS OF WRITING

Writing can seem at times an overwhelming drudgery, worse than scrubbing floors; at other moments, it's a sport full of thrills—like whizzing downhill on skis, not knowing what you'll meet around a bend. Surprising and unpredictable as the process may seem, nearly all writers do similar things:

- They generate ideas.
- They plan, draft, and develop their papers.
- They revise and edit.

Although these activities form the basis of most effective writing processes, they aren't lockstep stages: you don't always proceed in a straight line. You can skip around in whatever order you like, work on several parts at a time, or circle back over what's already done. For example, while gathering material, you may feel an urge to play with a sentence until it clicks. Or while writing a draft, you may decide to look for more material. You can leap ahead, cross out, backtrack, adjust, question, test a fresh approach, tinker, polish, and, at the end, spell-check the tricky words.

Generating Ideas

The first activity in writing—finding a topic and something to say about it—is often the most challenging and least predictable.

Finding Something to Write About. Selecting a topic is not always easy, but you may discover an idea while talking with friends, riding your bike, or even staring out the window. Sometimes a topic lies near home, in an everyday event you recall. Often your reading raises questions that call for investigation. When a particular writing assignment doesn't appeal to you, your challenge is to find a slant that does interest you. Find it, and words will flow—words that can engage readers as you accomplish your purpose. (See the graphic below.)

Discovering Material. You'll need information to shape and support your ideas—facts and figures, reports and opinions, examples and illustrations. Luckily you have numerous sources of supporting material to make your slant on a topic clear and convincing to your readers. You can recall your own experience and knowledge, you can observe things around you, you can converse with others who are knowledgeable, you can read materials that draw you to new views, and you can think critically about all the sources around you.

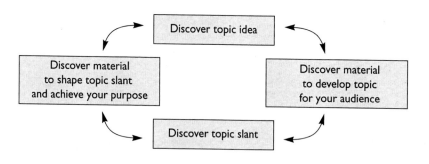

Planning, Drafting, and Developing

After finding a topic and beginning to gather material about it, you will plan your paper, write a draft, and then develop your ideas further. (See the graphic on the following page.)

Planning. Having discovered a burning idea (or at least a smoldering one) to write about, and some supporting material (but maybe not enough yet), you can sort out what matters most. If right away you see one main point, or thesis, for your paper, test various ways of stating it, given your audience and purpose:

MAYBE Parking in the morning before class is annoying.

OR Parking on campus is a big problem.

Next arrange your ideas and material in a sensible order that clarifies your point. For example, you might group and label the ideas you have

15

PLAN

- Identify your audience and purpose
- Decide on one main point
- State a thesis
- Organize ideas by grouping or outlining

DEVELOP

- Explain, analyze, and support
- Add examples, details, and definitions
- Supply evidence such as facts, statistics, expert testimony, and observations

DRAFT

- Start and restart
- Build paragraphs
- Open and conclude
- Create coherence

generated, make an outline, or analyze the main point, breaking it down into its parts:

> Parking on campus is a problem for students because of the long lines, inefficient entrances, and poorly marked spaces.

But if no clear thesis emerges quickly, don't worry. You may find one while you draft—that is, while you write an early version of your paper.

Drafting. When your ideas first start to flow, you want to welcome them—lure them forth, not tear them apart, so they don't go back into hiding. Don't be afraid to take risks at this stage: you'll probably be surprised and pleased at what happens, even though your first version will be rough. Writing takes time; a paper usually needs several drafts and may need a clearer introduction, a stronger conclusion, more convincing evidence, or a revised plan. Especially when your subject is unfamiliar or complicated, you may decide to throw out your first attempt and start over as a stronger idea evolves.

Developing. As you draft, you'll weave in explanations, examples, details, definitions, and varied evidence to make your ideas clear and persuasive. For example, you may need to define an at-risk student, illustrate the problems faced by a single parent, or supply statistics about hit-and-run accidents. If you lack specific support for your main point, you can use strategies for developing ideas, or return to strategies for generating ideas. You'll keep gaining insights and drawing conclusions while you draft. Welcome these ideas, and work them in if they fit.

Revising and Editing

You might want to relax once you have a draft, but for most writers revising begins the work in earnest. (See the visual below.) Revising means both reseeing and rewriting, making major changes so that your paper accomplishes what you want it to. After you have a well-developed and well-organized revision, you are ready to edit: to correct errors and improve wording.

Revising. Revision is more than just changing words. In fact, you may revise what you know and what you think while you're writing or when you pause to reread. You can then rework your thesis, reconsider your audience, shift your plans, decide what to put in or leave out, rearrange for clarity, move sentences or paragraphs around, connect points differently, or express ideas better. Perhaps you'll add costs to a paper on parking

REVISE	← PEER RESPONSE →	EDIT		PROOFREAD
• Purpose and thesis		• Word choice		• Spelling
• Audience		• Grammar		• Incorrect words
• Structure and support		• Sentences		• Missing words
• Emphasis		• Punctuation		• Minor errors
• Conciseness		• Mechanics		• Minor details
• Clarity		• Format for paper		

17

problems or switch to fathers instead of mothers as you consider teen parenthood.

If you put aside your draft for a few hours or a day, you can reread it with fresh eyes and a clear mind. Other students can also help you—sometimes more than a textbook or an instructor can—by responding to your drafts as engaged readers.

Editing. Editing means refining details and correcting flaws that stand in the way of your readers' understanding and enjoyment. Don't edit too early, though, because you may waste time on some part that you later revise out. In editing, you usually make these repairs:

- Get rid of unnecessary words.
- Choose livelier and more precise words.
- Replace any incorrect or inappropriate wording.
- Rearrange words in a clearer, more emphatic order.
- Combine short, choppy sentences, or break up long, confusing sentences.
- Refine transitions for continuity of thought.
- Check grammar, sentences, punctuation, and mechanics.

Proofreading. Finally you'll proofread your paper, taking a last look, checking correctness, and catching spelling or word-processing errors.

Remembering What Matters Most. Like a hard game of basketball, writing a college paper is strenuous. Without getting in your way, we want to lend you support and guidance throughout the writing process. So, no doubt, does your instructor, someone closer to you than a textbook writer. Still, even the best instructors and textbook writers—like the best coaches—can improve your game only so much. Advice on how to write won't make you a better writer. You'll learn more and have more fun when you take a few sentences to the hoop and make points yourself. After you sink a few baskets, you'll gain confidence in your ability and find the process of writing easier.

■ **ACTIVITY: Describing Your Writing Process**

Describe your writing process. How do you get started? How do you keep writing? What process do you go through to reach a final draft? Do your steps ever vary depending on the type of writing you're doing? What step or strategy in your writing process would you most like to change?

A SPOTLIGHT ON AUDIENCE AND PURPOSE

At any moment in the writing process, two questions are worth asking:

Who is my audience?   **Why am I writing?**

Writing for Readers

Your audience, or your readers, may or may not be defined in your assignment. Consider the following examples:

ASSIGNMENT 1   Discuss the advantages and disadvantages of home schooling.

ASSIGNMENT 2   In a letter to parents of school-aged children, discuss the advantages and disadvantages of home schooling.

If your assignment defines an audience, as the second example does, you will need to think about how to approach those readers and what to assume about their relationship to your topic. For example, what points would you include in a discussion aimed at parents? How would you organize your ideas? Would you discuss advantages or disadvantages first? On the other hand, how might your approach differ if the assignment read this way?

ASSIGNMENT 3   In a short article for a professional publication for teachers, discuss the advantages and disadvantages of home schooling.

When you analyze what readers know, believe, and value, you can aim your writing toward them with a better chance of hitting your mark. Use these questions to help you write and revise for your audience.

GENERAL AUDIENCE CHECKLIST

☐ Who are your readers? What is their relationship to you?

☐ What do your readers already know about this topic? What do you want them to learn?

☐ How much detail will they want to read about this topic?

(continued)

☐ What objections are they likely to raise as they read? How can you anticipate and overcome their objections?

☐ What's likely to convince them?

☐ What's likely to offend them?

■ **ACTIVITY: Considering Your Audience**

Write a short paragraph describing in detail a "worst" event—your worst date, worst dinner, worst car repair, or some similar catastrophe. Then revise that paragraph so that your audience is a person involved in the event—the person who went on that date with you, cooked or served the dinner, worked on your car. Now revise the paragraph again, this time writing to a person you plan to date soon, a cook at a restaurant you want to try, or a repair person working at another garage. Compare the three paragraphs. How are they similar? How do they differ?

Targeting Academic Readers

Although your future writing is likely to be aimed at a specific audience—the marketing team at work or the other members of an animal rescue group—many of your college assignments will resemble the example labeled Assignment 1 (see the preceding page). Those assignments will assume that you are addressing general academic readers, represented by your instructor and possibly your classmates. General academic readers typically expect clear, logical writing that uses supporting evidence to explain, interpret, or persuade. In addition, the particular expectations of academic audiences may differ by field. For example, biologists might assume you'll supply the findings from your experiment while literature specialists might look for plenty of relevant quotations from the novel you're analyzing. Depending on the field, your readers may expect certain topics, types of evidence, and approaches. Use these questions to help you pinpoint what your college readers expect.

ACADEMIC AUDIENCE CHECKLIST

☐ How has your instructor advised you to write for readers in the field? What criteria will be used for grading your papers?

(continued)

☐ What do the assigned readings in your course assume about readers and their expectations? Has your instructor recommended useful models or sample readings?

☐ What topics and issues concern readers in the field? What puzzles do they want to solve? How do they want to solve them?

☐ How is writing in the field commonly organized? For example, do writers tend to follow a persuasive pattern? That is, do they introduce the issue, state their assertion or claim, explain their reasons, acknowledge other views, and conclude? Do they use a series of conventional headings—for example, Abstract, Introduction to the Problem, Methodology, Findings, and Discussion?

☐ What evidence is typically gathered to support ideas or interpretations—facts and statistics, quotations from texts, summaries of research, references to authorities or prior studies, results from experimental research, or field notes from observations or interviews?

☐ What style, tone, and level of formality do writers in the field tend to use and readers tend to expect?

■ **ACTIVITY: Considering an Academic Audience**

Working by yourself or with a small group, use the preceding checklist to examine several reading or writing assignments in one of your courses. Try to identify prominent features of writing in the field. Which of these characteristics probably would be expected in student papers? How might you adjust your writing to meet those expectations? How would an academic paper differ from writing on the same topic for a general audience—for example, a letter to the editor, a newspaper article, a consumer brochure, an explanation for middle school students, or a Web page?

Writing for a Reason

Most college writing assignments ask you to write for a definite reason. For example, you might be asked to take a stand on a controversial issue and to persuade your readers to respect your position. Be careful not to confuse the sources and strategies you apply in these assignments with your ultimate purpose for writing. "To compare and contrast two things" is not a very interesting purpose; "to compare and contrast two Web sites *in order to explain their differences*" implies a real reason for writing.

In most college writing, your ultimate purpose will be to explain something to your readers or to convince them of something.

To sharpen your concentration on your purpose, ask yourself from the start, What do I want to do? And, in revising, Did I do what I meant to do? You'll find that these practical questions can help you slice out irrelevant information and remove other barriers to getting your paper where you want it to go.

■ ACTIVITY: Considering Your Purpose

Return to the three paragraphs you wrote for the activity "Considering Your Audience." Write a sentence or two summing up your purpose in writing each paragraph. Given these three purposes, how might you revise the paragraphs?

PETER ELBOW [b. 1935]

Freewriting

Peter Elbow received his Ph.D. from Brandeis University in 1969. He
has taught at several universities, including M.I.T., the University of
Massachusetts at Amherst, and SUNY at Stony Brook, where he directed
the writing program. Having experienced the inability to write as a
graduate student, he has since written widely on the writing process.
Often attempting to demystify the process, Elbow offers practical
advice on achieving one's writing goals, tackling such issues as writer's
block, freewriting, and, for instructors, teaching and evaluating writing. His most well-known books include *Writing With Power: Techniques
for Mastering the Writing Process* (1981), *Embracing Contraries: Essays
on Learning and Teaching* (1986), *What Is English?* (1990), and, most
recently, *Being a Writer* (2002).

The essay "Freewriting" is taken from Elbow's revolutionary work
Writing Without Teachers (1973) and discusses the rules of freewriting,
which amount to not stopping and not editing as you go. Editing is
good to do once a piece of writing has been produced, but editing
while producing kills the writer's unique voice.

The most effective way I know to improve your writing is to do freewriting exercises regularly. At least three times a week. They are sometimes
called "automatic writing," "babbling," or "jabbering" exercises. The idea
is simply to write for ten minutes (later on, perhaps fifteen or twenty).
Don't stop for anything. Go quickly without rushing. Never stop to look
back, to cross something out, to wonder how to spell something, to wonder what word or thought to use, or to think about what you are doing. If
you can't think of a word or a spelling, just use a squiggle or else write,
"I can't think of it." Just put down something. The easiest thing is just to
put down whatever is in your mind. If you get stuck it's fine to write "I
can't think what to say, I can't think what to say" as many times as you
want; or to repeat the last word you wrote over and over again; or anything else. The only requirement is that you *never* stop.

Peter Elbow, "Freewriting" from *Writing Without Teachers* by Peter Elbow.
Copyright © 1973, 1998 by Peter Elbow. Used by permission of Oxford University
Press.

What happens to a freewriting exercise is important. It must be a piece of writing which, even if someone reads it, doesn't send any ripples back to you. It is like writing something and putting it in a bottle in the sea. The teacherless class helps your writing by providing maximum feedback. Freewritings help you by providing no feedback at all. When I assign one, I invite the writer to let me read it. But I also tell him to keep it if he prefers. I read it quickly and make no comments at all and I do not speak with him about it. The main thing is that a freewriting must never be evaluated in any way; in fact there must be no discussion or comment at all.

Here is an example of a fairly coherent exercise (sometimes they are very incoherent, which is fine):

I think I'll write what's on my mind, but the only thing on my mind right now is what to write for ten minutes. I've never done this before and I'm not prepared in any way—the sky is cloudy today, how's that? now I'm afraid I won't be able to think of what to write when I get to the end of the sentence—well, here I am at the end of the sentence—here I am again, again, again, at least I'm still writing—Now I ask is there some reason to be happy that I'm still writing—ah yes! Here comes the question again — What am I getting out of this? What point is there in it? It's almost obscene to always ask it but I seem to question everything that way and I was gonna say something else pertaining to that but I got so busy writing down the first part that I forgot what I was leading into. This is kind of fun oh don't stop writing—cars and trucks speeding by somewhere out the window, pens clittering across peoples' papers. The sky is still cloudy—is it symbolic that I should be mentioning it? Huh? I dunno. Maybe I should try colors, blue, red, dirty words—wait a minute—no can't do that, orange, yellow, arm tired, green pink violet magenta lavender red brown black green—now that I can't think of any more colors—just about done—relief? maybe.

Freewriting may seem crazy but actually it makes simple sense. Think of the difference between speaking and writing. Writing has the advantage of permitting more editing. But that's its downfall too. Almost everybody interposes a massive and complicated series of editings between the time words start to be born into consciousness and when they finally come off the end of the pencil or typewriter onto the page. This is partly because schooling makes us obsessed with the "mistakes" we make in writing. Many people are constantly thinking about spelling and grammar as they try to write. I am always thinking about the awkwardness, wordiness, and general mushiness of my natural verbal product as I try to write down words.

But it's not just "mistakes" or "bad writing" we edit as we write. We 5
also edit unacceptable thoughts and feelings, as we do in speaking. In
writing there is more time to do it so the editing is heavier: when speaking, there's someone right there waiting for a reply and he'll get bored or
think we're crazy if we don't come out with something. Most of the time
in speaking, we settle for the catch-as-catch-can way in which the words
tumble out. In writing, however, there's a chance to try to get them right.
But the opportunity to get them right is a terrible burden: you can work
for two hours trying to get a paragraph "right" and discover it's not right
at all. And then give up.

Editing, *in itself*, is not the problem. Editing is usually necessary if we
want to end up with something satisfactory. The problem is that editing
goes on *at the same time* as producing. The editor is, as it were, constantly looking over the shoulder of the producer and constantly fiddling
with what he's doing while he's in the middle of trying to do it. No wonder the producer gets nervous, jumpy, inhibited, and finally can't be
coherent. It's an unnecessary burden to try to think of words and also
worry at the same time whether they're the right words.

The main thing about freewriting is that it is *nonediting*. It is an exercise in bringing together the process of producing words and putting
them down on the page. Practiced regularly, it undoes the ingrained
habit of editing at the same time you are trying to produce. It will make
writing less blocked because words will come more easily. You will use
up more paper, but chew up fewer pencils.

Next time you write, notice how often you stop yourself from writing
down something you were going to write down. Or else cross it out after
it's written. "Naturally," you say, "it wasn't any good." But think for a
moment about the occasions when you spoke well. Seldom was it
because you first got the beginning just right. Usually it was a matter of a
halting or even garbled beginning, but you kept going and your speech
finally became coherent and even powerful. There is a lesson here for
writing: trying to get the beginning just right is a formula for failure—
and probably a secret tactic to make yourself give up writing. Make
some words, whatever they are, and then grab hold of that line and reel
in as hard as you can. Afterwards you can throw away lousy beginnings
and make new ones. This is the quickest way to get into good writing.

The habit of compulsive, premature editing doesn't just make writing
hard. It also makes writing dead. Your voice is damped out by all the
interruptions, changes, and hesitations between the consciousness and
the page. In your natural way of producing words there is a sound, a texture, a rhythm—a voice—which is the main source of power in your
writing. I don't know how it works, but this voice is the force that will
make a reader listen to you, the energy that drives the meanings through

his thick skull. Maybe you don't *like* your voice; maybe people have made fun of it. But it's the only voice you've got. It's your only source of power. You better get back into it, no matter what you think of it. If you keep writing in it, it may change into something you like better. But if you abandon it, you'll likely never have a voice and never be heard.

Freewritings are vacuums. Gradually you will begin to carry over into 10 your regular writing some of the voice, force, and connectedness that creep into those vacuums.

PETER ELBOW [b. 1935]

Desperation Writing

Peter Elbow received his Ph.D. from Brandeis University in 1969. He has taught at several universities, including M.I.T., the University of Massachusetts at Amherst, and SUNY at Stony Brook, where he directed the writing program. Having experienced the inability to write as a graduate student, he has since written widely on the writing process. Often attempting to demystify the process, Elbow offers practical advice on achieving one's writing goals, tackling such issues as writer's block, freewriting, and, for instructors, teaching and evaluating writing. His most well-known books include *Writing With Power: Techniques for Mastering the Writing Process* (1981), *Embracing Contraries: Essays on Learning and Teaching* (1986), *What Is English?* (1990), and, most recently, *Being a Writer* (2002).

The essay "Desperation Writing" is taken from Elbow's revolutionary work *Writing Without Teachers* (1973) and lays out a concrete process for writers who are panicked and muddled and unable to write. Above all, Elbow recommends, "just write and keep writing" whatever comes to mind, always circling back to the task at hand, and later picking out ideas that can be organized into something coherent.

I know I am not alone in my recurring twinges of panic that I won't be able to write something when I need to, I won't be able to produce coherent speech or thought. And that lingering doubt is a great hindrance to writing. It's a constant fog or static that clouds the mind. I never got out of its clutches till I discovered that it was possible to write something — not something great or pleasing but at least something usable, workable — when my mind is out of commission. The trick is that you have to do all your cooking out on the table: Your mind is incapable of doing any inside. It means using symbols and pieces of paper not as a crutch but as a wheelchair.

The first thing is to admit your condition: Because of some mood or event or whatever, your mind is incapable of anything that could be called thought. It can put out a babbling kind of speech utterance, it can put a simple feeling, perception or sort-of-thought into understandable

Peter Elbow, "Desperation Writing" from *Writing Without Teachers* by Peter Elbow. Copyright © 1973, 1998 by Peter Elbow. Used by permission of Oxford University Press, Inc.

(though terrible) words. But it is incapable of considering anything in relation to anything else. The moment you try to hold that thought or feeling up against some other to see the relationship, you simply lose the picture—you get nothing but buzzing lines or waving colors.

So admit this. Avoid anything more than one feeling, perception, or thought. Simply write as much as possible. Try simply to steer your mind in the direction or general vicinity of the thing you are trying to write about and start writing and keep writing.

Just write and keep writing. (Probably best to write on only one side of the paper in case you should want to cut parts out with scissors—but you probably won't.) Just write and keep writing. It will probably come in waves. After a flurry, stop and take a brief rest. But don't stop too long. Don't think about what you are writing or what you have written or else you will overload the circuit again. Keep writing as though you are drugged or drunk. Keep doing this till you feel you have a lot of material that might be useful; or, if necessary, till you can't stand it any more — even if you doubt that there's anything useful there.

Then take a pad of little pieces of paper—or perhaps 3 × 5 cards— and simply start at the beginning of what you were writing, and as you read over what you wrote, every time you come to any thought, feeling, perception, or image that could be gathered up into one sentence or one assertion, do so and write it by itself on a little sheet of paper. In short, you are trying to turn, say, ten or twenty pages of wandering mush into twenty or thirty hard little crab apples. Sometimes there won't be many on a page. But if it seems to you that there are none on a page, you are making a serious error—the same serious error that put you in this comatose state to start with. You are mistaking lousy, stupid, second-rate, wrong, childish, foolish, worthless ideas for no ideas at all. Your job is not to pick out *good* ideas but to pick out ideas. As long as you were conscious, your words will be full of things that could be called feelings, utterances, ideas—things that can be squeezed into one simple sentence. This is your job. Don't ask for too much.

After you have done this, take those little slips or cards, read through them a number of times—not struggling with them, simply wandering and mulling through them; perhaps shifting them around and looking through in various sequences. In a sense these are cards you are playing solitaire with, and the rules of this particular game permit shuffling the unused pile.

The goal of this procedure with the cards is to get them to distribute themselves in two or three or ten or fifteen different piles on your desk. You can get them to do this almost by themselves if you simply keep reading through them in different orders; certain cards will begin to feel like they go with other cards. I emphasize this passive, thoughtless mode

5

28

because I want to talk about desperation writing in its pure state. In practice, almost invariably at some point in the procedure, your sanity begins to return. It is often at this point. You actually are moved to have thoughts or—and the difference between active and passive is crucial here—to *exert* thought; to hold two cards together and *build* or *assert* a relationship. It is a matter of bringing energy to bear.

So you may start to be able to do something active with these cards, and begin actually to think. But if not, just allow the cards to find their own piles with each other by feel, by drift, by intuition, by mindlessness.

You have now engaged in the two main activities that will permit you to get something cooked out on the table rather than in your brain: writing out into messy words, summing up into single assertions, and even sensing relationships between assertions. You can simply continue to deploy these two activities.

If, for example, after the first round of writing, assertion-making, and 10 pile-making, your piles feel as though they are useful and satisfactory for what you are writing—paragraphs or sections or trains of thought— then you can carry on from there. See if you can gather each pile up into a single assertion. When you can, then put the subsidiary assertions of that pile into their best order to fit with that single unifying one. If you *can't* get the pile into one assertion, then take the pile as the basis for doing some more writing out into words. In the course of this writing, you may produce for yourself the single unifying assertion you were looking for; or you may have to go through the cycle of turning the writing into assertions and piles and so forth. Perhaps more than once. The pile may turn out to want to be two or more piles itself; or it may want to become part of a pile you already have. This is natural. This kind of meshing into one configuration, then coming apart, then coming together and meshing into a different configuration—this is growing and cooking. It makes a terrible mess, but if you can't do it in your head, you have to put up with a cluttered desk and a lot of confusion.

If, on the other hand, all that writing *didn't* have useful material in it, it means that your writing wasn't loose, drifting, quirky, jerky, associative enough. This time try especially to let things simply remind you of things that are seemingly crazy or unrelated. Follow these odd associations. Make as many metaphors as you can—be as nutty as possible— and explore the metaphors themselves—open them out. You may have all your energy tied up in some area of your experience that you are leaving out. Don't refrain from writing about whatever else is on your mind: how you feel at the moment, what you are losing your mind over, randomness that intrudes itself on your consciousness, the pattern on the wallpaper, what those people you see out the window have on their minds—though keep coming back to the whateveritis you are supposed

29

to be writing about. Treat it, in short, like ten-minute writing exercises. Your best perceptions and thoughts are always going to be tied up in whatever is really occupying you, and that is also where your energy is. You may end up writing a love poem—or a hate poem—in one of those little piles while the other piles will finally turn into a lab report on data processing or whatever you have to write about. But you couldn't, in your present state of having your head shot off, have written that report without also writing the poem. And the report will have some of the juice of the poem in it and vice versa.

BRIAN DOYLE

Joyas Voladoras

From Portland, Oregon, **Brian Doyle** is a widely published essayist and self-proclaimed "traffick[er] in ideas and words." Doyle is known primarily for his work as the editor of *Portland Magazine*, a quarterly publication of the University of Portland. His writings have appeared in a variety of publications, including *Harper's*, the *American Scholar*, and the *Atlantic Monthly*, and have been anthologized in both *Best American Essays* and *Best Spiritual Writing*. Doyle, an Irish Catholic, is the author of various essay and short story collections including *The Wet Engine: Exploring the Mad Wild Miracle of the Heart* (2004), a book of reflections on his son's heart surgeries, and *The Grail: A Year Ambling and Shambling through an Oregon Vineyard in Pursuit of the Best Pinot Noir Wine in the Whole Wild World* (2006), a finalist for the Oregon Book Award. Doyle's other works include *Credo: Essays on Grace, Altar Boys, Bees, Kneeling, Saints, the Mass, Priests, Strong Women, Epiphanies, a Wake, and the Haunting Thin Energetic Dusty Figure of Jesus the Christ* (1999), *Leaping: Revelations and Epiphanies* (2003), and *Mink River* (2010).

"Joyas Voladoras," published in the *American Scholar* and excerpted from *The Wet Engine*, is also the name Spanish explorers attributed to hummingbirds—"flying jewels," that is—when first encountered in the Americas. In this prose poem, Doyle eloquently paints a portrait of the hummingbird and the blue whale, contrasting the animals' sizes and heartbeats, weaving together biology, lyrical imagery, and philosophy as he explores the heart as a metaphor for the human condition.

Consider the hummingbird for a long moment. A hummingbird's heart beats ten times a second. A hummingbird's heart is the size of a pencil eraser. A hummingbird's heart is a lot of the hummingbird. *Joyas volardores,* flying jewels, the first white explorers in the Americas called them, and the white men had never seen such creatures, for hummingbirds came into the world only in the Americas, nowhere else in the universe, more than three hundred species of them whirring and zooming and nectaring in hummer time zones nine times removed from ours, their

Brian Doyle, "Joyas Voladoras." From the *American Scholar*, Volume 73, No. 4, Autumn 2004. Copyright © 2004 by the author. Reprinted by permission of the author.

hearts hammering faster than we could clearly hear if we pressed our elephantine ears to their infinitesimal chests.

Each one visits a thousand flowers a day. They can dive at sixty miles an hour. They can fly backwards. They can fly more than five hundred miles without pausing to rest. But when they rest they come close to death: on frigid nights, or when they are starving, they retreat into torpor, their metabolic rate slowing to a fifteenth of their normal sleep rate, their hearts sludging nearly to a halt, barely beating, and if they are not soon warmed, if they do not soon find that which is sweet, their hearts grow cold, and they cease to be. Consider for a moment those hummingbirds who did not open their eyes again today, this very day, in the Americas: bearded helmet-crests and booted racket-tails, violet-tailed sylphs and violet-capped wood-nymphs, crimson topazes and purple-crowned fairies, red-tailed comets and amethyst woodstars, rainbow-bearded thornbills and glittering-bellied emeralds, velvet-purple coronets and golden-bellied star-frontlets, fiery-tailed awlbills and Andean hillstars, spatuletails and pufflegs, each the most amazing thing you have never seen, each thunderous wild heart the size of an infant's fingernail, each mad heart silent, a brilliant music stilled.

Hummingbirds, like all flying birds but more so, have incredible enormous immense ferocious metabolisms. To drive those metabolisms they have race-car hearts that eat oxygen at an eye-popping rate. Their hearts are built of thinner, leaner fibers than ours. Their arteries are stiffer and more taut. They have more mitochondria in their heart muscles—anything to gulp more oxygen. Their hearts are stripped to the skin for the war against gravity and inertia, the mad search for food, the insane idea of flight. The price of their ambition is a life closer to death; they suffer heart attacks and aneurysms and ruptures more than any other living creature. It's expensive to fly. You burn out. You fry the machine. You melt the engine. Every creature on earth has approximately two billion heartbeats to spend in a lifetime. You can spend them slowly, like a tortoise, and live to be two hundred years old, or you can spend them fast, like a hummingbird, and live to be two years old.

The biggest heart in the world is inside the blue whale. It weighs more than seven tons. It's as big as a room. It *is* a room, with four chambers. A child could walk around in it, head high, bending only to step through the valves. The valves are as big as the swinging doors in a saloon. This house of a heart drives a creature a hundred feet long. When this creature is born it is twenty feet long and weighs four tons. It is waaaaay bigger than your car. It drinks a hundred gallons of milk from its mama every day and gains two hundred pounds a day and when it is seven or eight years old it endures an unimaginable puberty and then it essentially disappears from human ken, for next to nothing is known of the mating habits, travel patterns, diet, social life, language, social structure, diseases, spirituality, wars, stories, despairs, and arts of the blue whale. There are perhaps ten thousand blue whales in the world, living in every ocean on earth, and of the largest mammal who ever lived we know nearly nothing. But we know this: the animals with the largest hearts in the world generally travel in pairs, and their penetrating moaning cries, their piercing yearning tongue, can be heard underwater for miles and miles.

Mammals and birds have hearts with four chambers. Reptiles and turtles 5 have hearts with three chambers. Fish have hearts with two chambers. Insects and mollusks have hearts with one chamber. Worms have hearts with one chamber, although they may have as many as eleven single-chambered hearts. Unicellular bacteria have no hearts at all; but even they have fluid eternally in motion, washing from one side of the cell to the other, swirling and whirling. No living being is without interior liquid motion. We all churn inside.

So much held in a heart in a lifetime. So much held in a heart in a day, an hour, a moment. We are utterly open with no one, in the end—not mother and father, not wife or husband, not lover, not child, not friend. We open windows to each but we live alone in the house of the heart. Perhaps we must. Perhaps we could not bear to be so naked, for fear of a constantly harrowed heart. When young we think there will come one person who will savor and sustain us always; when we are older we know this is the dream of a child, that all hearts finally are bruised and scarred, scored and torn, repaired by time and will, patched by force of character, yet fragile and rickety forevermore, no matter how ferocious the defense and how many bricks you bring to the wall. You can brick up your heart as stout and tight and hard and cold and impregnable as you possibly can and down it comes in an instant, felled by a woman's second glance, a child's apple breath, the shatter of glass in the road, the words I have something to tell you, a cat with a broken spine dragging itself into the forest to die, the brush of your mother's papery ancient hand in the thicket of your hair, the memory of your father's voice early in the morning echoing from the kitchen where he is making pancakes for his children.

[2004]

FIROOZEH DUMAS [b. 1966]

Hot Dogs and Wild Geese

At the age of seven, **Firoozeh Dumas** moved with her family from Abadan, Iran, to Whittier, California. Dumas's father, a former Fulbright Scholar, assured his family of his mastery of the English language and American culture, though—as Dumas quickly discovered—he had mastered neither. Her memoir, *Funny in Farsi* (2003), relays the amusing stories of her family's acclimation to their new home. A finalist for the 2004 PEN/USA award, the 2005 Audie Award for best audiobook, and the 2005 Thurber prize for American Humor, *Funny in Farsi* was also on the best-seller lists of the *San Francisco Chronicle* and the *Los Angeles Times*. Dumas's one-woman show, "Laughing without an Accent," opened in northern California in April 2005.

In "Hot Dogs and Wild Geese," from *Funny in Farsi*, Dumas wittily describes the difficulties her family had learning English after moving to America.

Moving to America was both exciting and frightening, but we found great comfort in knowing that my father spoke English. Having spent years regaling us with stories about his graduate years in America, he had left us with the distinct impression that America was his second home. My mother and I planned to stick close to him, letting him guide us through the exotic American landscape that he knew so well. We counted on him not only to translate the language but also to translate the culture, to be a link to this most foreign of lands. He was to be our own private Rosetta stone.

Once we reached America, we wondered whether perhaps my father had confused his life in America with someone else's. Judging from the bewildered looks of store cashiers, gas station attendants, and waiters, my father spoke a version of English not yet shared with the rest of America. His attempts to find a "vater closet" in a department store would usually lead us to the drinking fountain or the home furnishings section. Asking my father to ask the waitress the definition of "sloppy Joe" or "Tater Tots" was no problem. His translations, however, were

Firoozeh Dumas, "Hot Dogs and Wild Geese" from *Funny in Farsi*. Copyright © 2003 by Firoozeh Dumas. Reprinted by permission of Villard Books, a division of Random House, Inc.

highly suspect. Waitresses would spend several minutes responding to my father's questions, and these responses, in turn, would be translated as "She doesn't know." Thanks to my father's translations, we stayed away from hot dogs, catfish, and hush puppies, and no amount of caviar in the sea would have convinced us to try mud pie.

We wondered how my father had managed to spend several years attending school in America yet remain so utterly befuddled by Americans. We soon discovered that his college years had been spent mainly in the library, where he had managed to avoid contact with all Americans except his engineering professors. As long as the conversation was limited to vectors, surface tension, and fluid mechanics, my father was Fred Astaire with words. But one step outside the scintillating world of petroleum engineering and he had two left tongues.

My father's only other regular contact in college had been his roommate, a Pakistani who spent his days preparing curry. Since neither spoke English but both liked curries, they got along splendidly. The person who had assigned them together had probably hoped they would either learn English or invent a common language for the occasion. Neither happened.

My father's inability to understand spoken English was matched only by his efforts to deny the problem. His constant attempts at communicating with Americans seemed at first noble and adventurous, then annoying. Somewhere between his thick Persian accent and his use of vocabulary found in pre–World War II British textbooks, my father spoke a private language. That nobody understood him hurt his pride, so what he lacked in speaking ability, he made up for by reading. He was the only person who actually read each and every document before he signed it. Buying a washing machine from Sears might take the average American thirty minutes, but by the time my father had finished reading the warranties, terms of contracts, and credit information, the store was closing and the janitor was asking us to please step aside so he could finish mopping the floor.

My mother's approach to learning English consisted of daily lessons with Monty Hall and Bob Barker. Her devotion to *Let's Make a Deal* and *The Price Is Right* was evident in her newfound ability to recite useless information. After a few months of television viewing, she could correctly tell us whether a coffeemaker cost more or less than $19.99. How many boxes of Hamburger Helper, Swanson's TV dinners, or Turtle Wax could one buy without spending a penny more than twenty dollars? She knew that, too. Strolling down the grocery aisle, she rejoiced in her celebrity sightings—Lipton tea! Campbell's tomato soup! Betty Crocker Rich & Creamy Frosting! Every day, she would tell us the day's wins and losses on the game shows. "He almost won the boat, but the wife picked curtain number two and they ended up with a six-foot chicken statue." The bad

35

prizes on *Let's Make a Deal* sounded far more intriguing than the good ones. Who would want the matching La-Z-Boy recliners when they could have the adult-size crib and high-chair set?

My mother soon decided that the easiest way for her to communicate with Americans was to use me as an interpreter. My brother Farshid, with his schedule full of soccer, wrestling, and karate, was too busy to be recruited for this dubious honor. At an age when most parents are guiding their kids toward independence, my mother was hanging on to me for dear life. I had to accompany her to the grocery store, the hairdresser, the doctor, and every place else that a kid wouldn't want to go. My reward for doing this was the constant praise of every American we encountered. Hearing a seven-year-old translate Persian into English and vice versa made quite an impression on everyone. People lavished compliments on me. "You must be very, very, smart, a genius maybe." I always responded by assuring them that if they ever moved to another country, they, too, would learn the language. (What I wanted to say was that I wished I could be at home watching *The Brady Bunch* instead of translating the qualities of various facial moisturizers.) My mother had her own response to the compliments: "Americans are easily impressed."

I always encouraged my mother to learn English, but her talents lay elsewhere. Since she had never learned English in school, she had no idea of its grammar. She would speak entire paragraphs without using any verbs. She referred to everyone and everything as "it," leaving the listener wondering whether she was talking about her husband or the kitchen table. Even if she did speak a sentence more or less correctly, her accent made it incomprehensible. "W" and "th" gave her the most difficulty. As if God were playing a linguistic joke on us, we lived in "Vee-tee-er" (Whittier), we shopped at "Veetvood" (Whitwood) Plaza, I attended "Leffingvell" School, and our neighbor was none other than "Valter Villiams."

Despite little progress on my mother's part, I continually encouraged her. Rather than teach her English vocabulary and grammar, I eventually decided to teach her entire sentences to repeat. I assumed that once she got used to speaking correctly, I could be removed, like training wheels, and she would continue coasting. I was wrong.

Noticing some insects in our house one day, my mother asked me to call the exterminator. I looked up the number, then told my mother to call and say, "We have silverfish in our house." My mother grumbled, dialed the number, and said, "Please come rrright a-vay. Goldfeeesh all over dee house." The exterminator told her he'd be over as soon as he found his fishing pole.

A few weeks later, our washing machine broke. A repairman was summoned and the leaky pipe was quickly replaced. My mother wanted to

10

know how to remove the black stain left by the leak. "Y'all are gonna hafta use some elbow grease," he said. I thanked him and paid him and walked with my mother to the hardware store. After searching fruitlessly for elbow grease, I asked the salesclerk for help. "It removes stains," I added. The manager was called.

Once the manager finished laughing, he gave us the disappointing explanation. My mother and I walked home empty-handed. That, I later learned, is what Americans call a wild-goose chase.

Now that my parents have lived in America for thirty years, their English has improved somewhat, but not as much as one would hope. It's not entirely their fault; English is a confusing language. When my father paid his friend's daughter the compliment of calling her homely, he meant she would be a great housewife. When he complained about horny drivers, he was referring to their tendency to honk. And my parents still don't understand why teenagers want to be cool so they can be hot.

I no longer encourage my parents to learn English. I've given up. Instead, I'm grateful for the wave of immigration that has brought Iranian television, newspapers, and supermarkets to America. Now, when my mother wants to ask the grocer whether he has any more eggplants in the back that are a little darker and more firm, because the ones he has out aren't right for *khoresht bademjun*, she can do so in Persian, all by herself. And for that, I say hallelujah, a word that needs no translation.

[2003]

FRANZ KAFKA [1883-1924]

Before the Law

Franz Kafka was one of the major fiction writers of the 20th century. He was born to a middle class, German-speaking Jewish family in Prague, Austria-Hungary, presently the Czech Republic. His unique body of writing—much of which is incomplete—was mainly published posthumously. His stories, such as "The Metamorphosis" (1915), and novels, including *The Trial* (1925) and *The Castle* (1926), concern troubled individuals in a nightmarishly impersonal and bureaucratic world. This parable is from *The Trial*.

Before the law stands a doorkeeper. A man from the country comes to this doorkeeper and asks for admittance to the Law. But the doorkeeper informs him he cannot grant admittance at this time. The man ponders this and then asks if he will be allowed in later.

It is possible," says the doorkeeper, "but not at the moment." Since the gate stands open, as usual, and the doorkeeper steps to one side, the man stoops to peer through the gateway into the interior.

Observing that, the doorkeeper laughs and says: "If you are so drawn to it, just try to go in despite my interdiction. But take note: I am powerful. And I am only the least of the door-keepers. From hall to hall there is one doorkeeper after another, each more powerful than the last. The third doorkeeper is already so terrible that even I cannot bear to look at him."

These are difficulties the man from the country has not expected; the Law, he thinks, should be accessible at all times and to everyone, but as he now takes a closer look at the doorkeeper in his fur coat, with his big sharp nose and long, thin, black Tartar beard, he decides that it is better to wait until he gets permission to enter.

The doorkeeper gives him a stool and lets him sit down at one side of the door. There he sits for days and years. He makes many attempts to be admitted, and exhausts the doorkeeper with his pleas. The doorkeeper frequently has little interviews with him, asking him questions about his home and many other things, but the questions are put indifferently, as great lords put them, and always finish with the statement that he cannot be let in "yet."

The man, who came well equipped with many things for his journey, sacrifices all he has, however valuable, to bribe the doorkeeper. The doorkeeper accepts everything, but always with the remark: "I am only taking it to keep you from thinking you have omitted anything."

During these many years the man fixes his attention almost continuously on the doorkeeper. He forgets the other doorkeepers, and this first one seems to him the sole obstacle preventing access to the Law. He curses his miserable fate, in his early years boldly and loudly, later, as he grows old, he only grumbles to himself. He becomes childish, and since in his yearlong contemplation of the doorkeeper he has come to know even the fleas in his fur collar, he begs the fleas as well to help him and to change the doorkeeper's mind. At length his eyesight begins to fail, and he does not know whether the world is really darker or whether his eyes are only deceiving him. Yet even in the darkness he is aware of a radiance that streams unendingly from the gateway of the Law.

Now the man from the country does not have very long to live. Before he dies, all his experiences in these long years gather themselves in his head to one point, a question he has not yet asked the doorkeeper. He waves him nearer, since he can no longer raise his stiffening body. The doorkeeper has to bend low towards him, for the difference in height between them has altered much to the man's disadvantage.

"So, what do you still want to know?" asks the doorkeeper; "you are insatiable."

"Surely everyone strives to reach the Law," says the man, "so how does it happen that for all these many years no one but me has ever begged for admittance?"

The doorkeeper recognizes that the man has reached his end, and in order to penetrate his failing senses, he roars these words in his ear: "No one else could ever be admitted here, since this gate was made only for you. Now I am going to shut it."

ZHUANGZI [369-298 BCE]

The Parable of the Unusual Man

Zhuangzi (Chuang-Tzu) is ranked among the greatest of literary and philosophical giants that China has produced. Zhuangzi was born during the Warring States Era (403-221 BCE), more than a century after the death of Confucius. During this time, the ostensibly ruling house of Zhou had lost its authority, and there was increasing violence between states contending for imperial power. This situation gave birth to the phenomenon known as the "Hundred Schools". This was a flourishing of many schools of thought, each articulating its own conception of a return to a state of harmony.

In Wei there was an ugly man named Ai T'ai-t'o. But when men were around him, they thought only of him and couldn't break away, and when women saw him, they ran begging to their fathers and mothers, saying, `I'd rather be this gentleman's concubine than another man's wife!' - there were more than ten such cases and it hasn't stopped yet. No one ever heard him take the lead - he always just chimed in with other people. He wasn't in the position of a ruler where he could save men's lives, and he had no store of provisions to fill men's bellies. On top of that, he was ugly enough to astound the whole world, chimed in but never led, and knew no more than what went on right around him. And yet men and women flocked to him. He certainly must be different from other men, I thought, and I summoned him so I could have a look.

Just as they said - he was ugly enough to astound the world. But he hadn't been with me more than a month or so when I began to realize what kind of man he was, and before the year was out, I really trusted him. There was no one in the state to act as chief minister, and I wanted to hand the government over to him. He was vague about giving an answer, evasive, as though he hoped to be let off, and I was embarrassed, but in the end I turned the state over to him. Then, before I knew it, he left me and went away. I felt completely crushed, as though I'd suffered a loss and didn't have anyone left to enjoy my state with.

What kind of man is he anyway?

Lit. for Character

Comparison and Contrast

USING THE METHOD

An insomniac watching late-night television faces a choice between two World War II movies broadcasting at the same time. To make up his mind, he uses the dual method of comparison and contrast.

- **Comparison** shows the similarities between two or more subjects: the similar broadcast times and topics of the two movies force the insomniac to choose between them.
- **Contrast** shows the differences between subjects: the different actors, locations, and reputations of the two movies make it possible for the insomniac to choose one.

As in this example, comparison and contrast usually work together because any subjects that warrant side-by-side examination usually resemble each other in some respects and differ in others. (Since comparison and contrast are so closely related, the terms *comparison* and *compare* will be used from now on to designate both.)

You'll generally write a comparison for one of two purposes:

- To explain the similarities and differences between subjects so as to make either or both of them clear—an explanatory comparison.
- To evaluate subjects so as to establish their advantages and disadvantages, strengths and weaknesses—an evaluative comparison.

The explanatory comparison does not take a position on the relative merits of the subjects; the evaluative comparison does, and it usually concludes with a preference or a suggested course of action. In an explanatory

Jane E. Aaron, *40 Model Essays: A Portable Anthology*, pages 202–208. Copyright © 2005 by Bedford/St. Martin's.

comparison you might show how new income-tax laws differ from old laws. In an evaluative comparison on the same subject, you might argue that the old laws were more equitable than the new ones are.

Whether explanatory or evaluative, comparisons treat two or more subjects in the same general class or group: tax laws, religions, attitudes toward marriage, diseases, advertising strategies, diets, contact sports, friends. You may define the class to suit your interest—for instance, you might focus on Tuesday night's television shows, on network news programs, or on old situation comedies. The class likeness ensures that the subjects share enough features to make comparison worthwhile. With subjects from different classes, such as an insect and a tree, the similarities are so few and differences so numerous—and both are so obvious— that explaining them would be pointless.

In writing a comparison, you not only select subjects from the same class but also, using division, identify the features shared by the subjects. These **points of comparison** are the attributes of the class and thus of the subjects within the class. For instance, the points of comparison for diets may be forbidden foods, allowed foods, speed of weight loss, and nutritional quality; for air pollutants they may be sources and dangers to plants, animals, and humans. These points help you arrange similarities and differences between subjects, and, more important, they ensure direct comparison rather than a random listing of unrelated characteristics.

evaluation

In an effective comparison, a thesis or controlling idea governs the choice of class, points of comparison, and specific similarities and differences, while also making the comparison worthwhile for the reader. The thesis of an evaluative comparison generally emerges naturally because it coincides with the writer's purpose of supporting a preference for one subject over another:

thesis

THESIS SENTENCE (EVALUATION) The two diets result in similarly rapid weight loss, but Harris's requires much more self-discipline and is nutritionally much riskier than Marconi's.

In an explanatory comparison, however, the thesis does more than merely reflect the general purpose of explaining. It should go beyond the obvious and begin to identify the points of comparison. For example:

Thesis explanatory

TENTATIVE THESIS SENTENCE (EXPLANATION) Rugby and American football are the same in some respects and different in others.

REVISED THESIS SENTENCE (EXPLANATION) Though rugby requires less strength and more stamina than American football, the two games are very much alike in their rules and strategies.

These examples suggest other decisions you must make when writing a comparison:

- Should the subjects be treated in equal detail, or should one be emphasized over the others? Generally, give the subjects equal emphasis when they are equally familiar or are being evaluated (as the diets are in the previous example). Stress one subject over the others when it is less familiar (as rugby is in this country).
- Should the essay focus on similarities or differences, or both? Generally, stress them equally when all the points of comparison are equally familiar or important. Stress the differences between subjects usually considered similar (such as diets) or the similarities between subjects usually considered different (such as rugby and American football).

With two or more subjects, several points of comparison, many similarities and differences, and a particular emphasis, comparison clearly requires a firm organizational hand. You have two options for arranging a comparison:

- **Subject-by-subject,** in which you group the points of comparison under each subject so that the *subjects* are covered one at a time.
- **Point-by-point,** in which you group the subjects under each point of comparison so that the *points* are covered one at a time.

The following brief outlines illustrate the different arrangements as they might be applied to diets:

Subject-by-subject

Harris's diet
   Speed of weight loss
   Required self-discipline
   Nutritional risk
Marconi's diet
   Speed of weight loss
   Required self-discipline
   Nutritional risk

Point-by-point

Speed of weight loss
   Harris's diet
   Marconi's diet
Required self-discipline
   Harris's diet
   Marconi's diet
Nutritional risk
   Harris's diet
   Marconi's diet

Because the subject-by-subject arrangement presents each subject as a coherent unit, it is particularly useful for comparing impressions of subjects: the dissimilar characters of two friends, for instance. However, covering the subjects one at a time can break an essay into discrete pieces and strain readers' memories, so this arrangement is usually confined to essays that are short or that compare several subjects briefly. For longer papers requiring precise treatment of the individual points of comparison—say, an evaluation of two proposals for a new student-aid policy—the point-by-point arrangement is more useful. Its chief disadvantage is that the reader can get lost in details and fail to see any subject as a whole. Because each arrangement has its strengths and weaknesses, you may sometimes combine the two in a single work, using the divided arrangement to introduce or summarize overall impressions of the subjects and using the alternating arrangement to deal specifically with the points of comparison.

DEVELOPING AN ESSAY BY COMPARISON AND CONTRAST

Getting Started

Whenever you observe similarities or differences between two or more members of the same general class—activities, people, ideas, things, places—you have a possible subject for comparison and contrast. Just be sure that the subjects are worth comparing and that you can do the job in the space and time allowed. For instance, if you have a week to complete a three-page paper, don't try to show all the similarities and differences between country-and-western music and rhythm-and-blues. The effort can only frustrate you and irritate your readers. Instead, limit the subjects to a manageable size—for instance, the lyrics of a representative song in each type of music—so that you can develop the comparisons completely and specifically.

To generate ideas for a comparison, explore each subject separately to pick out its characteristics, and then explore the subjects together to see what characteristics one suggests for the other. Look for points of comparison. Early on, you can use division to identify points of comparison by breaking the subjects' general class into its elements. A song lyric, for instance, could be divided into story line or plot, basic emotion, and special language such as dialect or slang. After you have explored your subjects fully, you can use classification to group your characteristics under the points of comparison. For instance, you might classify characteristics of two proposals for a new student-aid policy into qualifications for aid, minimum and maximum amounts to be made available, and repayment terms.

While you are shaping your ideas, you should begin formulating your controlling idea, your thesis. As discussed earlier, in "Using the Method," the thesis should reflect your answers to these questions:

- Do the ideas suggest an explanatory or evaluative comparison?
- If explanatory, what point will the comparison make so that it does not merely recite the obvious?

- If evaluative, what preference or recommendation will you express?
- Will you emphasize both subjects equally or stress one over the other?
- Will you emphasize differences or similarities, or both?

As you gain increasing control over your material, consider also the needs of your readers:

- Do they know your subjects well, or should you take special care to explain one or both of them?
- Will your readers be equally interested in similarities and differences, or will they find one more enlightening than the other?
- If your essay is evaluative, are your readers likely to be biased against your preference? If so, you will need to support your case with plenty of specific reasons.

Most readers know intuitively how a comparison works, so they will expect you to balance your comparison feature for feature. In other words, all the features you mention for the first subject should be mentioned as well for the second, and any features not mentioned for the first subject should not suddenly materialize for the second.

Organizing

Your readers' needs and expectations can also help you plan your essay's organization. An effective introduction to a comparison essay often provides some context for readers—the situation that prompts the comparison, for instance, or the need for the comparison. Placing your thesis sentence in the introduction also informs readers of your purpose and point, and it may help keep you focused while you write.

For the body of the essay, choose the arrangement that will present your material most clearly and effectively. Remember that the subject-by-subject arrangement suits brief essays that compare dominant impressions of the subjects, whereas the point-by-point arrangement suits longer essays that require emphasis on the individual points of comparison. If you are torn between the two—wanting both to sum up each subject and to show the two side by side—then a combined arrangement may be your wisest choice.

A rough outline like the models for the diet comparison can help you plan the basic arrangement of your essay and also the order of the subjects and points of comparison. If your subjects are equally familiar to your readers and equally important to you, then it may not matter which subject you treat first, even in a subject-by-subject arrangement. But if one subject is less familiar or if you favor one, then that one should probably come second. You can also arrange the points themselves to reflect their importance and your readers' knowledge: from least to most significant or complex, from most to least familiar. Be sure to use the same order for both subjects.

The conclusion to a comparison essay can help readers see the whole picture: the chief similarities and differences between two subjects compared in a divided arrangement, or the chief characteristics of subjects compared in an alternating arrangement. In addition, you may want to comment on the significance of your comparison, advise readers on how they can use the information you have provided, or recommend a specific course of action for them to follow. As with all other methods of development, the choice of conclusion should reflect the impression you want to leave with readers.

Drafting

Drafting your essay gives you the chance to spell out your comparison so that it supports your thesis or, if your thesis is still tentative, to find your idea by writing into it. You can use paragraphs to help manage the comparison as it unfolds:

- In a subject-by-subject arrangement, if you devote two paragraphs to the first subject, try to do the same for the second subject. For both subjects, try to cover the points of comparison in the same order and group the same ones in paragraphs.
- In a point-by-point arrangement, balance the paragraphs as you move back and forth between subjects. If you treat several points of comparison for the first subject in one paragraph, do the same for the second subject. If you apply a single point of comparison to both subjects in one paragraph, do the same for the next point of comparison.

This way of drafting will help you achieve balance in your comparison and see where you may need more information to flesh out your subjects and your points. If the finished draft seems to march too rigidly in its pattern, you can always loosen things up when revising.

Revising and Editing

When you are revising and editing your draft, use the following questions to be certain that your essay meets the principal requirements of the comparative method.

- *Are your subjects drawn from the same class?* The subjects must have notable differences *and* notable similarities to make comparison worthwhile—though, of course, you may stress one group over the other.

- *Does your essay have a clear purpose and say something significant about the subject?* Your purpose of explaining or evaluating and the point you are making should be evident in your thesis *and* throughout the essay. A vague, pointless comparison will quickly bore readers.

- *Do you apply all points of comparison to both subjects?* Even if you emphasize one subject, the two subjects must match feature for feature. An unmatched comparison may leave readers with unanswered questions or weaken their confidence in your authority.

- *Does the pattern of comparison suit readers' needs and the complexity of the material?* Although readers will appreciate a clear organization and roughly equal treatment of your subjects and points of comparison, they will also appreciate some variety in the way you move back and forth. You don't have to devote a sentence to each point, first for one subject and then for the other, or alternate subjects sentence by sentence through several paragraphs. Instead, you might write a single sentence on one point or subject but four sentences on the other—if that's what your information requires.

BRUCE CATTON [1899–1978]

Grant and Lee:
A Study in Contrasts

Bruce Catton was born in Petoskey, Michigan, where his father was
a Congregational minister and headmaster of Benzonia Academy.
Catton began his studies at Oberlin College in 1916, but left without
graduating to serve in the U.S. Navy in World War I. Following his
brief military service, Catton worked as a newspaper reporter until
1941. He then became the Director of Information for the U.S. War
Production Board, eventually also working in the Department of Commerce and the Department of the Interior. His first book, *War Lords of
Washington* (1948), led to a new career as an amateur Civil War histo-
rian and author. *A Stillness at Appomattox* (1953), the third in Catton's
trilogy about the Army of the Potomac, earned him the National Book
Award and the Pulitzer Prize. His two other trilogies highlight the
social, political, and economic climate of the Civil War and Ulysses S.
Grant, respectively. In 1954, Catton was one of the founders of *American Heritage* magazine, and he served as senior editor from 1959 until
his death in 1978. In 1959, Harry S. Truman presented Catton with an
award for "meritorious service in the field of Civil War history" and
in 1976 Gerald R. Ford honored Catton with the Presidential Medal
of Freedom.

In "Grant and Lee: A Study in Contrasts," taken from *The American
Story* (1956), Catton's comparison of Robert E. Lee and Ulysses S.
Grant differentiates these two valorous generals by their social and
cultural backgrounds—Lee, devoted to old-world ideals of the landed
nobility, sought the preservation of the leisure class, while Grant, a
consummate frontiersman, reveled in the opportunities offered in a
democratic society.

When Ulysses S. Grant and Robert E. Lee met in the parlor of a modest
house at Appomattox Court House, Virginia, on April 9, 1865, to work
out the terms for the surrender of Lee's Army of Northern Virginia, a
great chapter in American life came to a close, and a great new chapter
began.

Bruce Catton, "Grant and Lee: A Study in Contrasts" from *The American Story*, edited
by Earl Schenck Miers. Reprinted by permission of the U.S. Capitol Historical Society.

These men were bringing the Civil War to its virtual finish. To be sure, other armies had yet to surrender, and for a few days the fugitive Confederate government would struggle desperately and vainly, trying to find some way to go on living now that its chief support was gone. But in effect it was all over when Grant and Lee signed the papers. And the little room where they wrote out the terms was the scene of one of the poignant, dramatic contrasts in American history.

They were two strong men, these oddly different generals, and they represented the strengths of two conflicting currents that, through them, had come into final collision.

Back of Robert E. Lee was the notion that the old aristocratic concept might somehow survive and be dominant in American life.

Lee was tidewater Virginia, and in his background were family, cul- 5 ture, and tradition...the age of chivalry transplanted to a New World which was making its own legends and its own myths. He embodied a way of life that had come down through the age of knighthood and the English country squire. America was a land that was beginning all over again, dedicated to nothing much more complicated than the rather hazy belief that all men had equal rights and should have an equal chance in the world. In such a land Lee stood for the feeling that it was somehow of advantage to human society to have a pronounced inequality in the social structure. There should be a leisure class, backed by ownership of land; in turn, society itself should be keyed to the land as the chief source of wealth and influence. It would bring forth (according to this ideal) a class of men with a strong sense of obligation to the community; men who lived not to gain advantage for themselves, but to meet the solemn obligations which had been laid on them by the very fact that they were privileged. From them the country would get its leadership; to them it could look for the higher values—of thought, of conduct, of personal deportment—to give it strength and virtue.

Lee embodied the noblest elements of this aristocratic ideal. Through him, the landed nobility justified itself. For four years, the Southern states had fought a desperate war to uphold the ideals for which Lee stood. In the end, it almost seemed as if the Confederacy fought for Lee; as if he himself was the Confederacy...the best thing that the way of life for which the Confederacy stood could ever have to offer. He had passed into legend before Appomattox. Thousands of tired, underfed, poorly clothed Confederate soldiers, long since past the simple enthusiasm of the early days of the struggle, somehow considered Lee the symbol of everything for which they had been willing to die. But they could not quite put this feeling into words. If the Lost Cause, sanctified by so much heroism and so many deaths, had a living justification, its justification was General Lee.

Grant, the son of a tanner on the Western frontier, was everything Lee was not. He had come up the hard way and embodied nothing in particular except the eternal toughness and sinewy fiber of the men who grew up beyond the mountains. He was one of a body of men who owed reverence and obeisance to no one, who were self-reliant to a fault, who cared hardly anything for the past but who had a sharp eye for the future.

These frontier men were the precise opposites of the tidewater aristocrats. Back of them, in the great surge that had taken people over the Alleghenies and into the opening Western country, there was a deep, implicit dissatisfaction with a past that had settled into grooves. They stood for democracy, not from any reasoned conclusion about the proper ordering of human society, but simply because they had grown up in the middle of democracy and knew how it worked. Their society might have privileges, but they would be privileges each man had won for himself. Forms and patterns meant nothing. No man was born to anything, except perhaps to a chance to show how far he could rise. Life was competition.

Yet along with this feeling had come a deep sense of belonging to a national community. The Westerner who developed a farm, opened a shop, or set up in business as a trader, could hope to prosper only as his own community prospered—and his community ran from the Atlantic to the Pacific and from Canada down to Mexico. If the land was settled, with towns and highways and accessible markets, he could better himself. He saw his fate in terms of the nation's own destiny. As its horizons expanded, so did his. He had, in other words, an acute dollars-and-cents stake in the continued growth and development of his country.

And that, perhaps, is where the contrast between Grant and Lee 10 becomes most striking. The Virginia aristocrat, inevitably, saw himself in relation to his own region. He lived in a static society which could endure almost anything except change. Instinctively, his first loyalty would go to the locality in which that society existed. He would fight to the limit of endurance to defend it, because in defending it he was defending everything that gave his own life its deepest meaning.

The Westerner, on the other hand, would fight with an equal tenacity for the broader concept of society. He fought so because everything he lived by was tied to growth, expansion, and a constantly widening horizon. What he lived by would survive or fall with the nation itself. He could not possibly stand by unmoved in the face of an attempt to destroy the Union. He would combat it with everything he had, because he could only see it as an effort to cut the ground out from under his feet.

So Grant and Lee were in complete contrast, representing two diametrically opposed elements in American life. Grant was the modern man emerging; beyond him, ready to come on the stage, was the great age of steel and machinery, of crowded cities and a restless, burgeoning vitality. Lee might have ridden down from the old age of chivalry, lance in hand, silken banner fluttering over his head. Each man was the perfect champion of his cause, drawing both his strengths and his weaknesses from the people he led.

Yet it was not all contrast, after all. Different as they were—in background, in personality, in underlying aspiration—these two great soldiers had much in common. Under everything else, they were marvelous fighters. Furthermore, their fighting qualities were really very much alike.

Each man had, to begin with, the great virtue of utter tenacity and fidelity. Grant fought his way down the Mississippi Valley in spite of acute personal discouragement and profound military handicaps. Lee hung on in the trenches at Petersburg after hope itself had died. In each man there was an indomitable quality...the born fighter's refusal to give up as long as he can still remain on his feet and lift his two fists.

Daring and resourcefulness they had, too; the ability to think faster 15 and move faster than the enemy. These were the qualities which gave Lee the dazzling campaigns of Second Manassas and Chancellorsville and won Vicksburg for Grant.

Lastly, and perhaps greatest of all, there was the ability, at the end, to turn quickly from war to peace once the fighting was over. Out of the way these two men behaved at Appomattox came the possibility of a peace of reconciliation. It was a possibility not wholly realized, in the years to come, but which did, in the end, help the two sections to become one nation again...after a war whose bitterness might have seemed to make such a reunion wholly impossible. No part of either man's life became him more than the part he played in their brief meeting in the McLean house at Appomattox. Their behavior there put all succeeding generations of Americans in their debt. Two great Americans, Grant and Lee—very different, yet under everything very much alike. Their encounter at Appomattox was one of the great moments of American history.

PATRICK N. ALLITT   [b. 1958]

Should Undergraduates Specialize?

Patrick N. Allitt is a professor of history at Emory University in Atlanta. He is a graduate of Oxford University and holds a Ph.D. from the University of California–Berkeley. He is the author of several books, including *I'm the Teacher, You're the Student: A Semester in a University Classroom* (2004) and *Catholic Intellectuals and Conservative Politics in America* (1993).

The following essay, "Should Undergraduates Specialize?" appeared in the June 16, 2006 issue of the *Chronicle of Higher Education*, a publication read mainly by college instructors and administrators. In the essay, Allitt compares his own experience at Oxford University with the curriculum his American college-bound daughter will encounter.

I was a college freshman thirty-two years ago, in 1974. My daughter, Frances, is about to become a college freshman this fall. I went to the University of Oxford in England. She's going to Emory University in America, and her experience is going to be completely different. There are some obvious outward contrasts. I was a shabby pseudo-hippie with a tangle of crazy hair and no decent clothes. She's well dressed, groomed, and presentable. I had a fountain pen and a record player. She has a computer and an iPod.

The ideas and justifications surrounding these two college adventures differ sharply. I was a product of the British meritocratic system which, after World War II, had nationalized higher education. The governing idea was that intelligent people were a national asset and that the nation was investing wisely by educating them, no matter their social origins.

Every student's tuition was paid in full, and every student was given, in addition, a grant to cover living expenses, board, and lodging. Only very wealthy Britons had to pay more than a token sum toward their children's college education. My three years at Oxford cost my parents a total of about $400. In those days, however, only a very small minority of

Patrick N. Allitt, "Should Undergraduates Specialize?" from *The Chronicle of Higher Education*, June 16, 2006. Reprinted with permission of the author.

British kids went to any kind of college. Most dropped out of school on the day of their sixteenth birthday, breathed a great sigh of relief, and never thought about education again.

The only criterion for British university admission then was academic. Oxford and Cambridge held their own entrance exams, interviewed students who wrote good answers, and chose the best of the interviewees. My class at Hertford College, Oxford, consisted of ninety students, all of them academic achievers.

Right from the start, each of us studied, or "read," only one discipline;   5
mine was history. Half my friends read in other academic disciplines: physics, biochemistry, English, French, and so on. The other half read in vocational disciplines like medicine, law, and engineering. Central to the entire system was early specialization. Even the broadest curriculum choice, PPE (Philosophy, Politics, and Economics), consisted of just three elements.

Learning was organized through the tutorial system. Every week I and one other student met our tutor. He had assigned a paper the previous week, and we had spent the time reading widely in the relevant literature. One of us read his paper aloud to begin the tutorial, then the tutor rubbished it and told us, in blistering detail, what we should have written, and how we should have interpreted the readings. The tutors didn't show any delicate concern for our feelings.

Frances, by contrast, is entering a decentralized system. Here the assumption is that the person who gets the education is going to be its chief beneficiary and that, accordingly, she should bear the cost. As a member of the great American middle class, she belongs to a generation whose parents have been fretting about the cost of higher education from the moment they beheld their newborns. Paying your way through Emory or its sisters in the American college big leagues is almost certain to cost more than $150,000. It's also a system in which half or more of her generation of eighteen-year-olds enroll in some kind of postsecondary institution; she'll be one of literally millions of freshmen this fall.

Criteria for admission are diverse. Doing well in high school is still a terrific idea, and, bless her heart, Frances has. But ever since seventh grade her teachers and counselors have nudged her to perform community service, play music and competitive sports, act, publish poems, edit magazines, do internships in hospitals, and in a dozen other ways be extracurricular to give her an edge in college applications. Being a legacy or (as her case) the child of a professor certainly helps.

She will study the liberal arts. In practice that means a couple of science classes, a bit of math, a language, a social-science-methods course, a spot of history, some "health" (such as "Principles of Physical Education," which is the Emory meaning of PPE), something in the performing arts, and then the nine or ten courses of a typical major. None of those courses will be vocational, but ideally they'll make her a well-rounded individuals—mature, informed, and tolerant.

She will take classes containing from six to one hundred students. 10 Occasionally she'll have to write a paper, but she'll rarely have to read one aloud to her teacher. She'll be in discussion groups with professors and teaching assistants, all of whom have been trained in sensitivity and diversity. Counselors, tutors, and an array of considerate "campus life" helpers will surround her. After four years, she'll probably have to select a graduate school to pursue her vocation, buckling down there to more years of toil.

How do the two systems compare in the eyes of someone who has seen plenty of each? The great virtue of the British system, particularly the early specialization, was that it enabled us to learn one discipline really well, to become far more deeply engaged with it than was possible for our American counterparts. It gave a marvelous opportunity to students who already knew where they were going to pursue their ambitions without distraction. As an undergraduate, I was already studying historical theory and the philosophy of history, which here is deferred to graduate school.

Its great and equal drawback was that it forced some students to choose too soon, before they were ready. An old girlfriend thought she wanted to be a psychologist but decided after a year that it had been a terrible idea, and had to petition to switch into French, which detained her at college a year longer than the rest of us. The system assumed freshmen were grown-ups who knew their own minds. Anyone familiar with a crowd of seventeen- and eighteen-year-olds knows that assumption is not always dependable.

The great virtue of the American system is its breadth. How impressed I was, as a TA at Berkeley, to have undergraduates in my very first history discussion group mention a relevant insight from Freud that they had picked up in "Psych," or refer to Laffer Curves that they'd studied in "Econ." They made me feel a trifle narrow and parochial.

Then they handed in their papers and wrote their finals, and my feelings of inadequacy disappeared. The great American drawbacks revealed themselves: The students' writing was awful, and their knowledge utterly superficial. Their breadth was the breadth of rivers an inch deep. The experience also drove home to me the truth, verified hundreds of times since, that the study of history is simply far too difficult for most students.

There are pros and cons to both systems. Surely it's possible, now, to 15 combine the merits of each rather than putting up with their weaknesses.

I think more American colleges should offer the chance to specialize right from the outset to those students who want it. Bright young physicists who want only to study physics should be free to do so, without laboring through courses in art history that seem to them a waste of valuable time.

In the same way, students who already have a clear vocational objective at the age of eighteen should be able to pursue it at top schools. My own experience showed that most law and medical students at Oxford *wanted* to get busy in preparation for the careers they had chosen, and were glad to be able to do so. (Incidentally, it didn't make them philistines; they enjoyed literature and read widely in other disciplines, just as I read plenty of great novels and a little science, even though I didn't take classes in those areas.)

At the same time, the vast American system can maintain the liberal-arts option for those who prefer it and don't yet have a clear sense of direction. Students with the right frame of mind thrive on studying diverse subjects until they're ready, sometimes at age twenty or older, to make a stronger commitment. But let's get rid of the idea that liberal arts is for everyone. America's commitment to equality and to universal education is noble and invigorating. But it shouldn't mean that one size fits all.

JUDITH VIORST [b. 1931]

The Truth about Lying

Born in Newark, New Jersey, **Judith Viorst** is a poet, essayist, novelist, and best-selling children's book writer. A graduate of Rutgers University, Viorst began writing poetry in the late 1960s, publishing *The Village Square* (1965) and several other collections of poems. One of Viorst's children's books, *Alexander and the Terrible, Horrible, No Good, Very Bad Day* (1972), sold over two million copies and was later transformed into a musical. After nearly two decades of writing for children and adults, Viorst returned to school, taking courses at the Washington Psychoanalytic Institute. This study, along with her personal experience of psychoanalysis, helped to inspire *Necessary Losses* (1986), a popular and critical success. Combining theory, poetry, interviews, and anecdotes, Viorst approaches personal growth as a shedding of illusions. In commenting on her writing, Viorst states that her books are not intended to give advice: "I only give advice to my children, husband and personal friends. But I think it helps to understand that the losses of life, the experience of aging, are not part of a malevolent fate. They are part of the human condition." Among her numerous books are *Yes, Married: A Saga of Love and Complaint* (1972), *Imperfect Control: Our Lifelong Struggles with Power and Surrender* (1999), and *Grown-Up Marriage: What We Know, Wish We Had Known, and Still Need to Know about Being Married* (2003). Her recent work includes the playful compilation of poems *Unexpectedly Eighty: And Other Adaptations* (2010).

In "The Truth about Lying," Viorst approaches lying with delicacy and candor, carefully classifying the different types of lies we all encounter. Viorst demonstrates her concern with the "moral puzzles" associated with lying, but decides that she "can't present any ultimate conclusions, for too many people would promptly disagree," and instead invites opinions from her readers.

I've been wanting to write on a subject that intrigues and challenges me: the subject of lying. I've found it very difficult to do. Everyone I've talked

Judith Viorst, "The Truth about Lying." Originally appeared in *Redbook*. Copyright © 1981 by Judith Viorst. Reprinted by permission of Lescher & Lescher, Ltd. All rights reserved.

to has a quite intense and personal but often rather intolerant point of view about what we can—and can never *never*—tell lies about. I've finally reached the conclusion that I can't present any ultimate conclusions, for too many people would promptly disagree. Instead, I'd like to present a series of moral puzzles, all concerned with lying. I'll tell you what I think about them. Do you agree?

SOCIAL LIES

Most of the people I've talked with say that they find social lying acceptable and necessary. They think it's the civilized way for folks to behave. Without these little white lies, they say, our relationships would be short and brutish and nasty. It's arrogant, they say, to insist on being so incorruptible and so brave that you cause other people unnecessary embarrassment or pain by compulsively assailing them with your honesty. I basically agree. What about you?

Will you say to people, when it simply isn't true, "I like your new hairdo," "You're looking much better," "It's so nice to see you," "I had a wonderful time"?

Will you praise hideous presents and homely kids?

Will you decline invitations with "We're busy that night—so sorry we   5 can't come," when the truth is you'd rather stay home than dine with the So-and-sos?

And even though, as I do, you may prefer the polite evasion of "You really cooked up a storm" instead of "The soup"—which tastes like warmed-over coffee—"is wonderful," will you, if you must, proclaim it wonderful?

There's one man I know who absolutely refuses to tell social lies. "I can't play that game," he says; "I'm simply not made that way." And his answer to the argument that saying nice things to someone doesn't cost anything is, "Yes, it does—it destroys your credibility." Now, he won't, unsolicited, offer his views on the painting you just bought, but you don't ask his frank opinion unless you want *frank*, and his silence at those moments when the rest of us liars are muttering, "Isn't it lovely?" is, for the most part, eloquent enough. My friend does not indulge in what he calls "flattery, false praise and mellifluous comments." When others tell fibs he will not go along. He says that social lying is lying, that little white lies are still lies. And he feels that telling lies is morally wrong. What about you?

58

PEACE-KEEPING LIES

Many people tell peace-keeping lies; lies designed to avoid irritation or argument; lies designed to shelter the liar from possible blame or pain; lies (or so it is rationalized) designed to keep trouble at bay without hurting anyone.

I tell these lies at times, and yet I always feel they're wrong. I understand why we tell them, but still they feel wrong. And whenever I lie so that someone won't disapprove of me or think less of me or holler at me, I feel I'm a bit of a coward, I feel I'm dodging responsibility, I feel . . . guilty. What about you?

Do you, when you're late for a date because you overslept, say that 10 you're late because you got caught in a traffic jam?

Do you, when you forget to call a friend, say that you called several times but the line was busy?

Do you, when you didn't remember that it was your father's birthday, say that his present must be delayed in the mail?

And when you're planning a weekend in New York City and you're not in the mood to visit your mother, who lives there, do you conceal—with a lie, if you must—the fact that you'll be in New York? Or do you have the courage—or is it the cruelty?—to say, "I'll be in New York, but sorry—I don't plan on seeing you"?

(Dave and his wife Elaine have two quite different points of view on this very subject. He calls her a coward. She says she's being wise. He says she must assert her right to visit New York sometimes and not see her mother. To which she always patiently replies: "Why should we have useless fights? My mother's too old to change. We get along much better when I lie to her.")

Finally, do you keep the peace by telling your husband lies on the sub- 15 ject of money? Do you reduce what you really paid for your shoes? And in general do you find yourself ready, willing and able to lie to him when you make absurd mistakes or lose or break things?

"I used to have a romantic idea that part of intimacy was confessing every dumb thing that you did to your husband. But after a couple of years of that," says Laura, "have I changed my mind!"

And having changed her mind, she finds herself telling peace-keeping lies. And yes, I tell them too. What about you?

PROTECTIVE LIES

Protective lies are lies folks tell—often quite serious lies—because they're convinced that the truth would be too damaging. They lie because they feel there are certain human values that supersede the wrong of having lied. They lie, not for personal gain, but because they believe it's for the good of the person they're lying to. They lie to those they love, to those who trust them most of all, on the grounds that breaking this trust is justified.

They may lie to their children on money or marital matters.

They may lie to the dying about the state of their health.   20

They may lie about adultery, and not—or so they insist—to save their own hide, but to save the heart and the pride of the men they are married to.

They may lie to their closest friend because the truth about her talents or son or psyche would be—or so they insist—utterly devastating.

I sometimes tell such lies, but I'm aware that it's quite presumptuous to claim I know what's best for others to know. That's called playing God. That's called manipulation and control. And we never can be sure, once we start to juggle lies, just where they'll land, exactly where they'll roll.

And furthermore, we may find ourselves lying in order to back up the lies that are backing up the lie we initially told.

And furthermore—let's be honest—if conditions were reversed, we   25 certainly wouldn't want anyone lying to us.

Yet, having said all that, I still believe that there are times when protective lies must nonetheless be told. What about you?

If your Dad had a very bad heart and you had to tell him some bad family news, which would you choose: to tell him the truth or lie?

If your former husband failed to send his monthly child-support check and in other ways behaved like a total rat, would you allow your children—who believed he was simply wonderful—to continue to believe that he was wonderful?

If your dearly beloved brother selected a wife whom you deeply disliked, would you reveal your feelings or would you fake it?

And if you were asked, after making love, "And how was that for you?"   30 would you reply, if it wasn't too good, "Not too good"?

Now, some would call a sex lie unimportant, little more than social lying, a simple act of courtesy that makes all human intercourse run smoothly. And some would say all sex lies are bad news and unacceptably protective. Because, says Ruth, "a man with an ego that fragile doesn't need your lies—he needs a psychiatrist." Still others feel that sex lies are indeed protective lies, more serious than simple social lying, and yet at times they tell them on the grounds that when it comes to matters sexual, everybody's ego is somewhat fragile.

"If most of the time things go well in sex," says Sue, "I think you're allowed to dissemble when they don't. I can't believe it's good to say, 'Last night was four stars, darling, but tonight's performance rates only a half.'"

I'm inclined to agree with Sue. What about you?

TRUST-KEEPING LIES

Another group of lies are trust-keeping lies, lies that involve triangulation, with A (that's you) telling lies to B on behalf of C (whose trust you'd promised to keep). Most people concede that once you've agreed not to betray a friend's confidence, you can't betray it, even if you must lie. But I've talked with people who don't want you telling them anything that they might be called on to lie about.

"I don't tell lies for myself," says Fran, "and I don't want to have to tell 35 them for other people." Which means, she agrees, that if her best friend is having an affair, she absolutely doesn't want to know about it.

"Are you saying," her best friend asks, "that if I went off with a lover and I asked you to tell my husband I'd been with you, that you wouldn't lie for me, that you'd betray me?"

Fran is very pained but very adamant. "I wouldn't want to betray you, so . . . don't ask me."

Fran's best friend is shocked. What about you?

Do you believe you can have close friends if you're not prepared to receive their deepest secrets?

Do you believe you must always lie for your friends? 40

Do you believe, if your friend tells a secret that turns out to be quite immoral or illegal, that once you've promised to keep it, you must keep it?

And what if your friend were your boss—if you were perhaps one of the President's men—would you betray or lie for him over, say, Watergate?

As you can see, these issues get terribly sticky.

It's my belief that once we've promised to keep a trust, we must tell lies to keep it. I also believe that we can't tell Watergate lies. And if these two statements strike you as quite contradictory, you're right—they're quite contradictory. But for now they're the best I can do. What about you?

Some say that truth will out and thus you might as well tell the truth. 45 Some say you can't regain the trust that lies lose. Some say that even

61

though the truth may never be revealed, our lies pervert and damage our relationships. Some say . . . well, here's what some of them have to say.

"I'm a coward," says Grace, "about telling close people important, difficult truths. I find that I'm unable to carry it off. And so if something is bothering me, it keeps building up inside till I end up just not seeing them anymore."

"I lie to my husband on sexual things, but I'm furious," says Joyce, "that he's too insensitive to know I'm lying."

"I suffer most from the misconception that children can't take the truth," says Emily. "But I'm starting to see that what's harder and more damaging for them is being told lies, is not being told the truth."

"I'm afraid," says Joan, "that we often wind up feeling a bit of contempt for the people we lie to."

And then there are those who have no talent for lying.   50

"Over the years, I tried to lie," a friend of mine explained, "but I always got found out and I always got punished. I guess I gave myself away because I feel guilty about any kind of lying. It looks as if I'm stuck with telling the truth."

For those of us, however, who are good at telling lies, for those of us who lie and don't get caught, the question of whether or not to lie can be a hard and serious moral problem. I liked the remark of a friend of mine who said, "I'm willing to lie. But just as a last resort—the truth's always better."

"Because," he explained, "though others may completely accept the lie I'm telling, I don't."

I tend to feel that way too.

What about you?   55

[1981]

62

Reading and Analyzing Short Fiction

This section is a brief review of how to read and analyze short fiction. Be sure to read actively to think reflexively and critically about short stories. Ask yourself, what do you know about the author and subject matter? What are your expectations of the story based on the title or author's biography? Secondly, how have your experiences (past readings or life events) given you a distinctive perspective about the story? Read with pen in hand—don't rely on memory, and be sure to make a note of surprising connections you make.

THE ELEMENTS OF FICTION

The elements (methods) of fiction help set up your expectations for the story. The **plot** is the sequence/structure of action or events within the story. It is delivered in numerous ways. Look for chronological techniques like flashbacks, foreshadowing, and frame-stories. The traditional dramatic structure relies on exposition, complication, rising action, conflict, climax, falling action, and dénouement. However, the story may start in the middle of the action (en medias res) or demonstrate a higher understanding of the human condition at the end (like an epiphany). Also **characterization** is how figures in the story are rendered, so they may seem plausible, acceptable and even sympathetic to the reader. This is revealed through character actions, reactions, dialogue, and authorial comments/descriptions. The types of characters are dynamic (subject to change) or static (without change), and round (created so that the reader can see many facets of his/her personality) or flat (given just one side to their personality). The perspective or **point of view** of the story-teller shapes your perceptions as a reader as well. This point of view is labeled as 1st, 2nd, or 3rd person. There are degrees of 1st person narration—from reliable to unreliable (this is a matter of trust in the narrator). Additionally, there are varying degrees of 3rd person: the nonparticipant (the passive observer); method of central intelligence (limited perception as there are details this narrator does not know); the omniscient (wherein the narrator knows all details); finally, an authorial intrusion (when the narrator directly speaks to the reader).

Diction (word choice and tone) and the time of the story-telling promote these narrative effects. Additionally, a literary **theme** reveals a subtle comment on the human condition. In more complicated fiction, there is more of a feel than a message. The **setting** is the correspondence of the time and place to other elements of fiction creates the atmosphere. The setting of the story shapes one's perceptions (for example, historical periods or famous places). Finally, a **symbol** is something (specifically a noun—person, place or thing) that stands for not only itself, but also for other levels of association and importance. A public symbol is universally understood. An incidental symbol is subject to the interpretation of the reader and his/her perceptions. An allegory is usually signaled by a consistently symbolic plot. Remember, in short fiction, nothing is above your notice. All the included methodology should inform your analysis.

GLOSSARY OF LITERARY TERMS AND CONCEPTS

character: A person in a literary work. Characters in literary works are often said to be either flat or round. A *flat* character usually has a single out-standing trait and remains the same throughout the work; a *round* character may have several traits and develops or changes over the course of the work.

characterization: The means by which an author presents or develops a character in a literary work.

climax: The part of a story or play in which a crisis is reached and a resolution is usually achieved.

conflict: Tension or struggle between opposing forces or characters in a work. A story's plot often develops from a conflict that leads to a climax and resolution (see **climax** and **plot**).

diction: An author's choice of words.

figurative language: Language that uses figures of speech.

figure of speech: A nonliteral use of language to compare dissimilar things (see **simile, metaphor,** and **personification**).

foreshadowing: Arranging information or events in a story or play in such a way that they suggest or hint at later events.

image: A sensory impression—such as seeing, hearing, touching, smelling, or tasting—evoked by a writer's words.

imagery: The use of recurrent and related images to produce a certain effect in a work.

irony: A discrepancy or contradiction between what is said and what is meant or between what is expected to happen and what does happen.

metaphor: A figure of speech that states or implies a comparison between two dissimilar things, as in *He bulldozed his way through the crowd.* This metaphor compares a person's actions to the way a bulldozer pushes obstacles out of its path.

narrator: The person telling the story in a literary work. The narrator should be considered a character in the work; he or she is not necessarily the same as the author.

paradox: A statement that, at first, appears contradictory or absurd but actually contains an understandable truth.

personification: A metaphorical figure of speech in which an inanimate object is spoken of as if it were living or human—for example, *An envious moon peeked through the trees.*

plot: The pattern of events in a literary work. In most cases, plot is driven by the conflict within a character or between one or more characters (see **character** and **conflict**).

point of view: The perspective from which a work is narrated. In a work with a *first-person point of view*, a character identified in the work tells the story. In *a third-person point of view*, the author is implied as being the narrator.

protagonist: The main character in a literary work.

rhyme: Repetition of identical or similar sounds, as in *ache* and *break.*

rhythm: A pattern of recurrent qualities; usually stressed syllables, words, or sounds.

setting: The time and place in which the events of a literary work take place.

simile: A figure of speech using *like* or *as* to create a comparison between two unlike things, as in *He pushed through the crowd like a bulldozer.*

speaker: The named or imagined character or voice is speaking the words of a poem. The speaker of a poem is not the author but a persona created by the author to express the work.

stanza: A group of two or more lines in a poem.

structure: The overall design or organization of a work.

style: The manner in which an author uses language and other literary devices to tell a story.

symbol: A person, place, object, or set of events representing something beyond itself.

theme: The main or controlling idea in a literary work. A successful theme comments on the larger aspects of the human experience, not just the condition of an individual character in a literary work.

tone: The writer's attitude toward the characters, subject, and audience, as revealed through the language of his or her work.

GEORGE ORWELL [1903–1950]

A Hanging

Born in India in 1903, Eric Blair was the son of an English civil servant in the British Raj, the rule of India by the British, as was his father. Educated in England, Blair was an Imperial policeman in India for five years but resigned and returned to England to pursue his dream of becoming a writer, complete with a pen name, **George Orwell.** Known best for his novels *Animal Farm* (1945) and *1984* (1949), Orwell's political concerns were expressed in nonfiction as well, in works such as his chronicle of life among the poor, *Down and Out in Paris and London* (1933). Because of his stands against economic injustice and totalitarianism, Orwell remains an influential figure, as the adjectivization of his pen name shows—*Orwellian* has entered the vernacular as a term to describe the violence done to language and common sense by totalitarianism.

"A Hanging" details the execution of a Hindu prisoner at the hands of the British Raj. The brief piece is emotionally daunting and powerfully told; seemingly insignificant details come together to paint a bleak picture in which the life of a condemned prisoner is no more than an inconvenience. Stupefied by the actions and reactions of the prison warden and guards, Orwell, like the others, is eventually overcome with laughter—perhaps his only means of tolerating "the mystery, the unspeakable wrongness, of cutting a life short when it is in full tide."

It was in Burma, a sodden morning of the rains. A sickly light, like yellow tinfoil, was slanting over the high walls into the jail yard. We were waiting outside the condemned cells, a row of sheds fronted with double bars, like small animal cages. Each cell measured about ten feet by ten and was quite bare within except for a plank bed and a pot for drinking water. In some of them brown, silent men were squatting at the inner bars, with their blankets draped round them. These were the condemned men, due to be hanged within the next week or two.

George Orwell, "A Hanging" from *Shooting an Elephant and Other Essays* by George Orwell, copyright 1950 by Sonia Brownell Orwell and renewed 1978 by Sonia Pitt-Rivers. Reprinted by permission of Harcourt, Inc. CD-ROM reproduced by permission of AM Heath & Co. Ltd. on behalf of Bill Hamilton as the Literary Executor of the Estate of the Late Sonia Brownell Orwell and Martin Secker & Warburg Ltd.

One prisoner had been brought out of his cell. He was a Hindu, a puny wisp of a man, with a shaven head and vague liquid eyes. He had a thick, sprouting mustache, absurdly too big for his body, rather like the mustache of a comic man on the films. Six tall Indian warders were guarding him and getting him ready for the gallows. Two of them stood by with rifles and fixed bayonets, while the others handcuffed him, passed a chain through his handcuffs and fixed it to their belts, and lashed his arms tight to his sides. They crowded very close about him, with their hands always on him in a careful, caressing grip, as though all the while feeling him to make sure he was there. It was like men handling a fish which is still alive and may jump back into the water. But he stood quite unresisting, yielding his arms limply to the ropes, as though he hardly noticed what was happening.

Eight o'clock struck and a bugle call, desolately thin in the wet air, floated from the distant barracks. The superintendent of the jail, who was standing apart from the rest of us, moodily prodding the gravel with his stick, raised his head at the sound. He was an army doctor, with a grey toothbrush mustache and a gruff voice. "For God's sake, hurry up, Francis," he said irritably. "The man ought to have been dead by this time. Aren't you ready yet?"

Francis, the head jailer, a fat Dravidian in a white drill suit and gold spectacles, waved his black hand. "Yes sir, yes sir," he bubbled. "All iss satisfactorily prepared. The hangman iss waiting. We shall proceed."

"Well, quick march, then. The prisoners can't get their breakfast till 5 this job's over."

We set out for the gallows. Two warders marched on either side of the prisoner, with their rifles at the slope; two others marched close against him, gripping him by arm and shoulder, as though at once pushing and supporting him. The rest of us, magistrates and the like, followed behind. Suddenly, when we had gone ten yards, the procession stopped short without any order or warning. A dreadful thing had happened—a dog, come goodness knows whence, had appeared in the yard. It came bounding among us with a loud volley of barks and leapt round us wagging its whole body, wild with glee at finding so many human beings together. It was a large woolly dog, half Airedale, half pariah. For a moment it pranced around us, and then, before anyone could stop it, it had made a dash for the prisoner, and jumping up tried to lick his face. Everybody stood aghast, too taken aback even to grab the dog.

"Who let that bloody brute in here?" said the superintendent angrily. "Catch it, someone!"

A warder detached from the escort, charged clumsily after the dog, but it danced and gambolled just out of his reach, taking everything as part of the game. A young Eurasian jailer picked up a handful of gravel and tried to stone the dog away, but it dodged the stones and came after us again. Its yaps echoed from the jail walls. The prisoner, in the grasp of the two warders, looked on incuriously, as though this was another formality of the hanging. It was several minutes before someone managed to catch the dog. Then we put my handkerchief through its collar and moved off once more, with the dog still straining and whimpering.

It was about forty yards to the gallows. I watched the bare brown back of the prisoner marching in front of me. He walked clumsily with his bound arms, but quite steadily, with that bobbing gait of the Indian who never straightens his knees. At each step his muscles slid neatly into place, the lock of hair on his scalp danced up and down, his feet printed themselves on the wet gravel. And once, in spite of the men who gripped him by each shoulder, he stepped lightly aside to avoid a puddle on the path.

It is curious; but till that moment I had never realized what it means 10 to destroy a healthy, conscious man. When I saw the prisoner step aside to avoid the puddle, I saw the mystery, the unspeakable wrongness, of cutting a life short when it is in full tide. This man was not dying, he was alive just as we are alive. All the organs of his body were working— bowels digesting food, skin renewing itself, nails growing, tissues forming—all toiling away in solemn foolery. His nails would still be growing when he stood on the drop, when he was falling through the air with a tenth-of-a-second to live. His eyes saw the yellow gravel and the grey walls, and his brain still remembered, foresaw, reasoned—even about puddles. He and we were a party of men walking together, seeing, hearing, feeling, understanding the same world; and in two minutes, with a sudden snap, one of us would be gone—one mind less, one world less.

The gallows stood in a small yard, separate from the main grounds of the prison, and overgrown with tall prickly weeds. It was a brick erection like three sides of a shed, with planking on top, and above that two beams and a crossbar with the rope dangling. The hangman, a grey-haired convict in the white uniform of the prison, was waiting beside his machine. He greeted us with a servile crouch as we entered. At a word from Francis the two warders, gripping the prisoner more closely than ever, half led, half pushed him to the gallows and helped him clumsily up the ladder. Then the hangman climbed up and fixed the rope round the prisoner's neck.

We stood waiting, five yards away. The warders had formed in a rough circle round the gallows. And then, when the noose was fixed, the prisoner began crying out to his god. It was a high, reiterated cry of "Ram! Ram! Ram! Ram!" not urgent and fearful like a prayer or cry for help, but steady, rhythmical, almost like the tolling of a bell. The dog answered the sound with a whine. The hangman, still standing on the gallows, produced a small cotton bag like a flour bag and drew it down over the prisoner's face. But the sound, muffled by the cloth, still persisted, over and over again: "Ram! Ram! Ram! Ram! Ram!"

The hangman climbed down and stood ready, holding the lever. Minutes seemed to pass. The steady, muffled crying from the prisoner went on and on, "Ram! Ram! Ram!" never faltering for an instant. The superintendent, his head on his chest, was slowly poking the ground with his stick; perhaps he was counting the cries, allowing the prisoner a fixed number—fifty, perhaps, or a hundred. Everyone had changed colour. The Indians had gone grey like bad coffee, and one or two of the bayonets were wavering. We looked at the lashed, hooded man on the drop, and listened to his cries—each cry another second of life; the same thought was in all our minds; oh, kill him quickly, get it over, stop that abominable noise!

Suddenly the superintendent made up his mind. Throwing up his head he made a swift motion with his stick. "Chalo!" he shouted almost fiercely.

There was a clanking noise, and then dead silence. The prisoner had 15 vanished, and the rope was twisting on itself. I let go of the dog, and it galloped immediately to the back of the gallows; but when it got there it stopped short, barked, and then retreated into a corner of the yard, where it stood among the weeds, looking timorously out at us. We went round the gallows to inspect the prisoner's body. He was dangling with his toes pointed straight downwards, very slowly revolving, as dead as a stone.

The superintendent reached out with his stick and poked the bare brown body; it oscillated slightly. "*He's* all right," said the superintendent. He backed out from under the gallows, and blew out a deep breath. The moody look had gone out of his face quite suddenly. He glanced at his wrist-watch. "Eight minutes past eight. Well, that's all for this morning, thank God."

The warders unfixed bayonets and marched away. The dog, sobered and conscious of having misbehaved itself, slipped after them. We walked out of the gallows yard, past the condemned cells with their waiting prisoners, into the big central yard of the prison. The convicts, under the command of warders armed with lathis, were already receiving their breakfast. They squatted in long rows, each man holding a tin pannikin, while two warders with buckets marched around ladling out rice; it seemed quite a homely, jolly scene, after the hanging. An enormous relief had come upon us now that the job was done. One felt an impulse to sing, to break into a run, to snigger. All at once everyone began chattering gaily.

The Eurasian boy walking beside me nodded towards the way we had come, with a knowing smile: "Do you know, sir, our friend (he meant the dead man) when he heard his appeal had been dismissed, he pissed on the floor of his cell. From fright. Kindly take one of my cigarettes, sir. Do you not admire my new silver case, sir? From the boxwallah, two rupees eight annas. Classy European style."

Several people laughed—at what, nobody seemed certain.

Francis was walking by the superintendent, talking garrulously: "Well, 20 sir, all has passed off with the utmost satisfactoriness. It was all finished—flick! Like that. It iss not always so—oah, no! I have known cases where the doctor wass obliged to go beneath the gallows and pull the prisoner's legs to ensure decease. Most disagreeable!"

"Wriggling about, eh? That's bad," said the superintendent.

"Ach, sir, it iss worse when they become refractory! One man, I recall, clung to the bars of hiss cage when we went to take him out. You will scarcely credit, sir, that it took six warders to dislodge him, three pulling at each leg. We reasoned with him, 'My dear fellow,' we said, 'think of all the pain and trouble you are causing to us!' But no, he would not listen! Ach, he wass very troublesome!"

I found that I was laughing quite loudly. Everyone was laughing. Even the superintendent grinned in a tolerant way. "You'd better all come out and have a drink," he said quite genially. "I've got a bottle of whisky in the car. We could do with it."

We went through the big double gates of the prison into the road. "Pulling at his legs!" exclaimed a Burmese magistrate suddenly, and burst into a loud chuckling. We all began laughing again. At that moment Francis' anecdote seemed extraordinarily funny. We all had a drink together, native and European alike, quite amicably. The dead man was a hundred yards away.

GEORGE ORWELL [1903–1950]

Shooting an Elephant

Born in India in 1903, Eric Blair was the son of an English civil servant in the British Raj, the rule of India by the British, as was his father. Educated in England, Blair was an Imperial policeman in India for five years but resigned and returned to England to pursue his dream of becoming a writer, complete with a pen name, **George Orwell**. Known best for his novels *Animal Farm* (1945) and *1984* (1949), Orwell's political concerns were expressed in nonfiction as well, in works such as his chronicle of life among the poor, *Down and Out in Paris and London* (1933). Because of his stands against economic injustice and totalitarianism, Orwell remains an influential figure, as the adjectivization of his pen name shows—*Orwellian* has entered the vernacular as a term to describe the violence done to language and common sense by totalitarianism. "Shooting an Elephant" tells the story of a moment early in Orwell's life when his sense of injustice surfaced.

In Moulmein, in Lower Burma, I was hated by large numbers of people—the only time in my life that I have been important enough for this to happen to me. I was sub-divisional police officer of the town, and in an aimless, petty kind of way anti-European feeling was very bitter. No one had the guts to raise a riot, but if a European woman went through the bazaars alone somebody would probably spit betel juice over her dress. As a police officer I was an obvious target and was baited whenever it seemed safe to do so. When a nimble Burman tripped me up on the football field and the referee (another Burman) looked the other way, the crowd yelled with hideous laughter. This happened more than once. In the end the sneering yellow faces of young men that met me everywhere, the insults hooted after me when I was at a safe distance, got badly on my nerves. The young Buddhist priests were the worst of all. There were several thousands of them in the town and none of them

"Shooting an Elephant" from *Shooting an Elephant and Other Essays* by George Orwell. In the U.S., copyright © 1950 by Sonia Brownell Orwell and renewed 1978 by Sonia Pitt-Rivers. In Canada, copyright © 1936 by George Orwell. Reprinted by permission of Harcourt, Inc., Bill Hamilton as the Literary Executor of the Estate of the Late Sonia Brownell Orwell, and Secker & Warburg Ltd.

71

seemed to have anything to do except stand on street corners and jeer at Europeans.

All this was perplexing and upsetting. For at that time I had already made up my mind that imperialism was an evil thing and the sooner I chucked up my job and got out of it the better. Theoretically—and secretly, of course—I was all for the Burmese and all against their oppressors, the British. As for the job I was doing, I hated it more bitterly than I can perhaps make clear. In a job like that you see the dirty work of Empire at close quarters. The wretched prisoners huddling in the stinking cages of the lock-ups, the grey, cowed faces of the long-term convicts, the scarred buttocks of the men who had been flogged with bamboos— all these oppressed me with an intolerable sense of guilt. But I could get nothing into perspective. I was young and ill-educated and I had had to think out my problems in the utter silence that is imposed on every Englishman in the East. I did not even know that the British Empire is dying, still less did I know that it is a great deal better than the younger empires that are going to supplant it. All I knew was that I was stuck between my hatred of the empire I served and my rage against the evil-spirited little beasts who tried to make my job impossible. With one part of my mind I thought of the British Raj as an unbreakable tyranny, as something clamped down, in *saecula saeculorum* upon the will of prostrate peoples; with another part I thought that the greatest joy in the world would be to drive a bayonet into a Buddhist priest's guts. Feelings like these are the normal by-products of imperialism; ask any Anglo-Indian official, if you can catch him off duty.

One day something happened which in a roundabout way was enlightening. It was a tiny incident in itself, but it gave me a better glimpse than I had had before of the real nature of imperialism—the real motives for which despotic governments act. Early one morning the sub-inspector at a police station the other end of the town rang me up on the phone and said that an elephant was ravaging the bazaar. Would I please come and do something about it? I did not know what I could do, but I wanted to see what was happening and I got on to a pony and started out. I took my rifle, an old .44 Winchester and much too small to kill an elephant, but I thought the noise might be useful *in terrorem*. Various Burmans stopped me on the way and told me about the elephant's doings. It was not, of course, a wild elephant, but a tame one which had gone "must." It had been chained up, as tame elephants always are when their attack of "must" is due, but on the previous night it had broken its chain and escaped. Its mahout, the only person who could manage it when it was in that state, had set out in pursuit, but had taken the wrong direction and was now twelve hours' journey away, and in the morning the elephant had suddenly reappeared in the town. The Burmese population had no weapons and were quite helpless against it. It had already destroyed somebody's bamboo hut, killed a cow and raided some fruit-stalls and devoured the stock; also it had met the municipal rubbish van and, when the driver jumped out and took to his heels, had turned the van over and inflicted violences upon it.

The Burmese sub-inspector and some Indian constables were waiting for me in the quarter where the elephant had been seen. It was a very poor quarter, a labyrinth of squalid bamboo huts, thatched with palm-leaf, winding all over a steep hillside. I remember that it was a cloudy, stuffy morning at the beginning of the rains. We began questioning the people as to where the elephant had gone and, as usual, failed to get any definite information. That is invariably the case in the East; a story always sounds clear enough at a distance, but the nearer you get to the scene of events the vaguer it becomes. Some of the people said that the elephant had gone in one direction, some said that he had gone in an-other, some professed not even to have heard of any elephant. I had al-most made up my mind that the whole story was a pack of lies, when we heard yells a little distance away. There was a loud, scandalized cry of "Go away, child! Go away this instant!" and an old woman with a switch in her hand came round the corner of a hut, violently shooing away a crowd of naked children. Some more women followed, clicking their tongues and exclaiming; evidently there was something that the children ought not to have seen. I rounded the hut and saw a man's dead body sprawling in the mud. He was an Indian, a black Dravidian coolie, al-most naked, and he could not have been dead many minutes. The people said that the elephant had come suddenly upon him round the corner of the hut, caught him with its trunk, put its foot on his back and ground him into the earth. This was the rainy season and the ground was soft, and his face had scored a trench a foot deep and a couple of yards long. He was lying on his belly with arms crucified and head sharply twisted to one side. His face was coated with mud, the eyes wide open, the teeth bared and grinning with an expression of unendurable agony. (Never tell me, by the way, that the dead look peaceful. Most of the corpses I have seen looked devilish.) The friction of the great beast's foot had stripped the skin from his back as neatly as one skins a rabbit. As soon as I saw the dead man I sent an orderly to a friend's house nearby to borrow an elephant rifle. I had already sent back the pony, not wanting it to go mad with fright and throw me if it smelt the elephant.

The orderly came back in a few minutes with a rifle and five car- 5 tridges, and meanwhile some Burmans had arrived and told us that the elephant was in the paddy fields below, only a few hundred yards away. As I started forward practically the whole population of the quarter flocked out of the houses and followed me. They had seen the rifle and were all shouting excitedly that I was going to shoot the elephant. They had not shown much interest in the elephant when he was merely ravaging their homes, but it was different now that he was going to be shot. It was a bit of fun to them, as it would be to an English crowd; besides they wanted the meat. It made me vaguely uneasy. I had no intention of shooting the elephant—I had merely sent for the rifle to defend myself if necessary—and it is always unnerving to have a crowd following you. I marched down the hill, looking and feeling a fool, with the rifle over my shoulder and an ever-growing army of people jostling at my heels. At the bottom, when you got away from the huts, there was a metalled road and beyond that a miry waste of paddy fields a thousand yards across, not yet ploughed but soggy from the first rains and dotted with coarse grass. The elephant was standing eight yards from the road, his left side towards us. He took not the slightest notice of the crowd's approach. He was tearing up bunches of grass, beating them against his knees to clean them and stuffing them into his mouth.

I had halted on the road. As soon as I saw the elephant I knew with perfect certainty that I ought not to shoot him. It is a serious matter to shoot a working elephant—it is comparable to destroying a huge and costly piece of machinery—and obviously one ought not to do it if it can possibly be avoided. And at that distance, peacefully eating, the elephant looked no more dangerous than a cow. I thought then and I think now that his attack of "must" was already passing off; in which case he would merely wander harmlessly about until the mahout came back and caught him. Moreover, I did not in the least want to shoot him. I decided that I would watch him for a little while to make sure that he did not turn savage again, and then go home.

But at that moment I glanced round at the crowd that had followed me. It was an immense crowd, two thousand at the least and growing every minute. It blocked the road for a long distance on either side. I looked at the sea of yellow faces above the garish clothes—faces all happy and excited over this bit of fun, all certain that the elephant was going to be shot. They were watching me as they would watch a conjurer about to perform a trick. They did not like me, but with the magical rifle in my hands I was momentarily worth watching. And suddenly I realized that I should have to shoot the elephant after all. The people expected it of me and I had got to do it; I could feel their two thousand wills pressing me forward, irresistibly. And it was at this moment, as I stood there with the rifle in my hands, that I first grasped the hollowness, the futility of the white man's dominion in the East. Here was I, the white man with his gun, standing in front of the unarmed native crowd—seemingly the leading actor of the piece; but in reality I was only an absurd puppet pushed to and fro by the will of those yellow faces behind. I perceived in this moment that when the white man turns tyrant it is his own freedom that he destroys. He becomes a sort of hollow, posing dummy, the conventionalized figure of a sahib. For it is the condition of his rule that he shall spend his life in trying to impress the "natives," and so in every crisis he has got to do what the "natives" expect of him. He wears a mask, and his face grows to fit it. I had got to shoot the elephant. I had committed myself to doing it when I sent for the rifle. A sahib has got to act like a sahib; he has got to appear resolute, to know his own mind and do definite things. To come all that way, rifle in hand, with two thousand people marching at my heels, and then to trail feebly away, having done nothing—no, that was impossible. The crowd would laugh at me. And my whole life, every white man's life in the East, was one long struggle not to be laughed at.

But I did not want to shoot the elephant. I watched him beating his bunch of grass against his knees, with that preoccupied grandmotherly air that elephants have. It seemed to me that it would be murder to shoot him. At that age I was not squeamish about killing animals, but I had never shot an elephant and never wanted to. (Somehow it always seems worse to kill a *large* animal.) Besides, there was the beast's owner to be considered. Alive, the elephant was worth at least a hundred pounds; dead, he would only be worth the value of his tusks, five pounds, possibly. But I had got to act quickly. I turned to some experienced-looking Burmans who had been there when we arrived, and asked them how the elephant had been behaving. They all said the same thing: he took no notice of you if you left him alone, but he might charge if you went too close to him.

It was perfectly clear to me what I ought to do. I ought to walk up to within, say, twenty-five yards of the elephant and test his behavior. If he charged, I could shoot; if he took no notice of me, it would be safe to leave him until the mahout came back. But also I knew that I was going to do no such thing. I was a poor shot with a rifle and the ground was soft mud into which one would sink at every step. If the elephant charged and I missed him, I should have about as much chance as a toad under a steam-roller. But even then I was not thinking particularly of my own skin, only of the watchful yellow faces behind. For at that moment, with the crowd watching me, I was not afraid in the ordinary sense, as I would have been if I had been alone. A white man mustn't be frightened in front of "natives"; and so, in general, he isn't frightened. The sole thought in my mind was that if anything went wrong those two thousand Burmans would see me pursued, caught, trampled on and reduced to a grinning corpse like that Indian up the hill. And if that happened it was quite probable that some of them would laugh. That would never do. There was only one alternative. I shoved the cartridges into the magazine and lay down on the road to get a better aim.

The crowd grew very still, and a deep, low, happy sigh, as of people 10 who see the theatre curtain go up at last, breathed from innumerable throats. They were going to have their bit of fun after all. The rifle was a beautiful German thing with cross-hair sights. I did not then know that in shooting an elephant one would shoot to cut an imaginary bar running from ear-hole to ear-hole. I ought, therefore, as the elephant was sideways on, to have aimed straight at his ear-hole; actually I aimed several inches in front of this, thinking the brain would be further forward.

When I pulled the trigger I did not hear the bang or feel the kick—one never does when a shot goes home—but I heard the devilish roar of glee that went up from the crowd. In that instant, in too short a time, one would have thought, even for the bullet to get there, a mysterious, terrible change had come over the elephant. He neither stirred nor fell, but every line of his body had altered. He looked suddenly stricken, shrunken, immensely old, as though the frightful impact of the bullet had paralysed him without knocking him down. At last, after what seemed a long time—it might have been five seconds, I dare say—he sagged flabbily to his knees. His mouth slobbered. An enormous senility seemed to have settled upon him. One could have imagined him thousands of years old. I fired again into the same spot. At the second shot he did not collapse but climbed with desperate slowness to his feet and stood weakly upright, with legs sagging and head drooping. I fired a third time. That was the shot that did for him. You could see the agony of it jolt his whole body and knock the last remnant of strength from his legs. But in falling he seemed for a moment to rise, for as his hind legs collapsed beneath him he seemed to tower upward like a huge rock toppling, his trunk reaching skywards like a tree. He trumpeted, for the first and only time. And then down he came, his belly towards me, with a crash that seemed to shake the ground even where I lay.

I got up. The Burmans were already racing past me across the mud. It was obvious that the elephant would never rise again, but he was not dead. He was breathing very rhythmically with long rattling gasps, his great mound of a side painfully rising and falling. His mouth was wide open—I could see far down into caverns of pale pink throat. I waited a long time for him to die, but his breathing did not weaken. Finally I fired my two remaining shots into the spot where I thought his heart must be. The thick blood welled out of him like red velvet, but still he did not die. His body did not even jerk when the shots hit him, the tortured breathing continued without a pause. He was dying, very slowly and in great

76

agony, but in some world remote from me where not even a bullet could damage him further. I felt that I had got to put an end to that dreadful noise. It seemed dreadful to see the great beast lying there, powerless to move and yet powerless to die, and not even to be able to finish him. I sent back for my small rifle and poured shot after shot into his heart and down his throat. They seemed to make no impression. The tortured gasps continued as steadily as the ticking of a clock.

In the end I could not stand it any longer and went away. I heard later that it took him half an hour to die. Burmans were bringing dahs and baskets even before I left, and I was told they had stripped his body almost to the bones by the afternoon.

Afterwards, of course, there were endless discussions about the shooting of the elephant. The owner was furious, but he was only an Indian and could do nothing. Besides, legally I had done the right thing, for a mad elephant has to be killed, like a mad dog, if its owner fails to control it. Among the Europeans opinion was divided. The older men said I was right, the younger men said it was a damn shame to shoot an elephant for killing a coolie, because an elephant was worth more than any damn Coringhee coolie. And afterwards I was very glad that the coolie had been killed; it put me legally in the right and it gave me a sufficient pretext for shooting the elephant. I often wondered whether any of the others grasped that I had done it solely to avoid looking a fool.

[1950]

Lit. for Values

Cause-and-Effect Analysis

USING THE METHOD

Why did free agency become so important in professional baseball, and how has it affected the sport? What caused the recent warming of the Pacific Ocean, and how did the warming affect the earth's weather? We answer questions like these with **cause-and-effect analysis,** the method of dividing occurrences into their elements to find relationships among them. When we analyze **causes,** we discover which of the events preceding a specified outcome actually made it happen:

What caused Adolf Hitler's rise in Germany?

Why have herbal medicines become so popular?

When we analyze **effects,** we discover which of the events following a specified occurrence actually resulted from it:

What do we do for (or to) drug addicts when we imprison them?

What happens to our foreign policy when the president's advisers disagree over its conduct?

These are existing effects of past or current situations, but effects are often predicted for the future:

How would a cure for cancer affect the average life expectancy of men and women?

Jane E. Aaron, *40 Model Essays: A Portable Anthology*, pages 267–274. Copyright © 2005 by Bedford/St. Martin's.

How might your decision to major in history affect your job prospects?

Causes and effects can also be analyzed together, as the questions opening this section illustrate.

Cause-and-effect analysis is found in just about every discipline and occupation, including history, social science, natural science, engineering, medicine, law, business, and sports. In any of these fields, as well as in writing done for college courses, your purpose in analyzing may be to explain or to persuade. In explaining why something happened or what its outcome was or will be, you try to order experience and pin down the connections in it. In arguing with cause-and-effect analysis, you try to demonstrate why one explanation of causes is more accurate than another or how a proposed action will produce desirable or undesirable consequences.

The possibility of arguing about causes and effects points to the main challenge of this method. Related events sometimes overlap, sometimes follow one another immediately, and sometimes connect over gaps in time. They vary in their duration and complexity. They vary in their importance. Analyzing causes and effects thus requires not only identifying them but also discerning their relationships accurately and weighing their significance fairly.

Causes and effects often do occur in a sequence, each contributing to the next in what is called a **causal chain.** For instance, an unlucky man named Jones ends up in prison, and the causal chain leading to his imprisonment can be outlined as follows: Jones's neighbor, Smith, dumped trash on Jones's lawn. In reprisal, Jones set a small brushfire in Smith's yard. A spark from the fire accidentally ignited Smith's house. Jones was prosecuted for the fire and sent to jail. In this chain, each event is the cause of an effect, which in turn is the cause of another effect, and so on to the unhappy conclusion.

Identifying a causal chain partly involves sorting out events in time:

- **Immediate** causes or effects occur nearest an event. For instance, the immediate cause of a town's high unemployment rate may be the closing of a large manufacturing plant where many townspeople work.

- **Remote** causes or effects occur further away in time. The remote cause of the town's unemployment rate may be a drastic decline in the company's sales or (more remote) a weak regional or national economy.

Analyzing causes also requires distinguishing their relative importance in the sequence:

- **Major** causes are directly and primarily responsible for the outcome. For instance, if a weak economy is responsible for low sales, it is a major cause of the manufacturing plant's closing.
- **Minor** causes (also called **contributory** causes) merely contribute to the outcome. The manufacturing plant may have closed for the additional reason that the owners could not afford to make repairs to its machines.

As these examples illustrate, time and significance can overlap in cause-and-effect analysis: a weak economy, for instance, is both a remote and a major cause; the lack of funds for repairs is both an immediate and a minor cause.

Because most cause-and-effect relationships are complex, you should take care to avoid several pitfalls in analyzing and presenting them. One is a confusion of coincidence and cause—that is, an assumption that because one event preceded another, it must have caused the other. This error is nicknamed **post hoc,** from the Latin *post hoc, ergo propter hoc,* meaning "after this, therefore because of this." Superstitions often illustrate post hoc: a basketball player believes that a charm once ended her shooting slump, so she now wears the charm whenever she plays. But post hoc also occurs in more serious matters. For instance, the office of a school administrator is vandalized, and he blames the incident on a recent speech by the student-government president criticizing the administration. But the administrator has no grounds for his accusation unless he can prove that the speech incited the vandals. In the absence of proof, the administrator commits the error of post hoc by asserting that the speech caused the vandalism simply because the speech preceded the vandalism.

Another potential problem in cause-and-effect writing is **oversimplification.** You must consider not just the causes and effects that seem obvious or important but all the possibilities: remote as well as immediate, minor as well as major. One form of oversimplification confuses a necessary cause with a sufficient cause:

- A **necessary** cause, as the term implies, is one that must happen in order for an effect to come about; an effect can have more than one necessary cause. For example, if emissions from a factory cause a high rate of illness in a neighborhood, the emissions are a necessary cause.
- A **sufficient** cause, in contrast, is one that brings about the effect *by itself.* The emissions are not a sufficient cause of the illness rate unless all other possible causes—such as water pollution or infection—can be eliminated.

Oversimplification can also occur if you allow opinions or emotions to cloud the interpretation of evidence. Suppose that you are examining the reasons why a gun-control bill you opposed was passed by the state legislature. Some of your evidence strongly suggests that a member of the legislature, a vocal supporter of the bill, was unduly influenced by lobbyists. But if you attributed the passage of the bill solely to this legislator, you would be exaggerating the significance of a single legislator and you would be ignoring the opinions of the many others who also voted for the bill. To achieve a balanced analysis, you would have to put aside your own feelings and consider all possible causes for the bill's passage.

DEVELOPING AN ESSAY BY CAUSE-AND-EFFECT ANALYSIS

Getting Started

Assignments in almost any course or line of work ask for cause-and-effect analysis: What caused the Vietnam War? In the theory of sociobiology, what are the effects of altruism on the survival of the group? Why did costs exceed the budget last month? You can find your own subject for cause-and-effect analysis from your experiences, from observation of others, from your course work, or from your reading outside school. Anytime you find yourself wondering what happened or why or what if, you may be onto an appropriate subject.

Remember that your treatment of causes or effects or both must be thorough; thus your subject must be manageable within the constraints of time and space imposed on you. Broad subjects like those following must be narrowed to something whose complexities you can cover adequately.

BROAD SUBJECT	Causes of the increase in American industrial productivity
NARROWER SUBJECT	Causes of increasing productivity on one assembly line
BROAD SUBJECT	Effects of cigarette smoke
NARROWER SUBJECT	Effects of parents' secondhand smoke on small children

Whether your subject suggests a focus on causes or effects or both, list as many of them as you can from memory or from further reading. If the subject does not suggest a focus, then ask yourself questions to begin exploring it:

- Why did it happen?
- What contributed to it?

- What were or are its results?
- What might its consequences be?

One or more of these questions should lead you to a focus and, as you explore further, to a more complete list of ideas.

But you cannot stop with a simple list, for you must arrange the causes or effects in sequence and weigh their relative importance: Do the events sort out into a causal chain? Besides the immediate causes and effects, are there also less obvious, more remote ones? Besides the major causes or effects, are there also minor ones? At this stage, you may find that diagramming relationships helps you see them more clearly. The following diagram illustrates the earlier example of the plant closing:

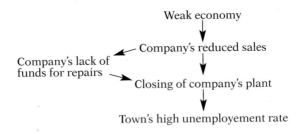

Though uncomplicated, the diagram does sort out the causes and effects and shows their relationships and sequence.

While you are developing a clear picture of your subject, you should also be anticipating the expectations and needs of your readers. As with the other methods of essay development, consider especially what your readers already know about your subject and what they need to be told:

- Do readers require background information?
- Are they likely to be familiar with some of the causes or effects you are analyzing, or should you explain every one completely?
- Which causes or effects might readers already accept?
- Which ones might they disagree with? If, for instance, the plant closing affected many of your readers—putting them or their relatives out of work—they might blame the company's owners rather than economic forces beyond the owners' control. You would have to address these preconceptions and provide plenty of evidence for your own interpretation.

To help manage your ideas and information, try to develop a thesis sentence that states your subject, your perspective on it, and your purpose.

The thesis sentence should reflect your judgments about the relative significance of possible causes or effects. For instance:

EXPLANATORY THESIS SENTENCE Being caught in the middle of a family quarrel has affected not only my feelings about my family but also my relations with friends.

PERSUASIVE THESIS SENTENCE Contrary to local opinion, the many people put out of work by the closing of Windsor Manufacturing were victims not of the owners' incompetence but of the nation's weak economy.

Organizing

The introduction to a cause-and-effect essay can pull readers in by describing the situation whose causes or effects you plan to analyze, such as the passage of a bill in the legislature or a town's high unemployment rate. The introduction may also provide background, such as a brief narrative of a family quarrel; or it may summarize the analysis of causes or effects that the essay disputes, such as the townspeople's blaming the owners for a plant's closing. If your thesis is not already apparent in the introduction, stating it explicitly can tell readers exactly what your purpose is and which causes or effects or both you plan to highlight. If you anticipate that readers will oppose your thesis, however, you may want to delay stating it until the end of the essay, after you have provided the evidence to support it.

The arrangement of the body of the essay depends primarily on your material and your emphasis. If events unfold in a causal chain with each effect becoming the cause of another effect, and if stressing these links coincides with your purpose, then a simple chronological sequence will probably be clearest. But if events overlap and vary in significance, their organization will require more planning. Probably the most effective way to arrange either causes or effects is in order of increasing importance. Such an arrangement helps readers see which causes or effects you consider minor and which major, while it also reserves your most significant (and probably most detailed) point for last. The groups of minor or major events may then fit into a chronological framework.

To avoid being preoccupied with organization while you are drafting your essay, prepare some sort of outline before you start writing. The outline need not be detailed so long as you have written the details elsewhere or can retrieve them easily from your mind. But it should show all the causes or effects you want to discuss and the order in which you will cover them.

To conclude your essay, you may want to restate your thesis — or state it, if you deliberately withheld it for the end — so that readers are left with the point of your analysis. If your analysis is complex, readers may also benefit from a summary of the relationships you have identified. And depending on your purpose, you may want to specify why your analysis is significant, what use your readers can make of it, or what action you hope they will take.

Drafting

While drafting your essay, strive primarily for clarity—sharp details, strong examples, concrete explanations. To make readers see not only *what* you see but also *why* you see it, you can draw on just about any method of developing a piece of writing. For instance, you might narrate the effect of a situation on one person, analyze a process, or compare and contrast two interpretations of cause. Particularly if your thesis is debatable (like the earlier example asserting the owners' blamelessness for the plant's closing), you will need accurate, representative facts to back up your interpretation, and you may also need quotations from experts such as witnesses and scholars. If you do not support your assertions specifically, your readers will have no reason to believe them.

Revising and Editing

While revising and editing your draft, consider the following questions to be sure your analysis is sound and clear.

- *Have you explained causes or effects clearly and specifically?* Readers will need to see the pattern of causes or effects—their sequence and relative importance. And readers will need facts, examples, and other evidence to understand and accept your analysis.

- *Have you demonstrated that causes are not merely coincidences?* Avoid the error of post hoc—of assuming that one event caused another just because it preceded the other. To be convincing, a claim that one event caused another must be supported with ample evidence.

- *Have you considered all the possible causes or effects?* Your analysis should go beyond what is most immediate or obvious so that you do not oversimplify the cause-and-effect relationships. Your readers will expect you to present the relationships in all their complexity.

- *Have you represented the cause-and-effect relationships honestly?* Don't deliberately ignore or exaggerate causes or effects in a misguided effort to strengthen your essay. If a cause fails to support your thesis but still does not invalidate it, mention the cause and explain why you believe it to be unimportant. If a change you are proposing will have bad effects as well as good, mention the bad effects and explain how they are outweighed by the good. As long as your reasoning and evidence are sound, such admissions will not weaken your essay; on the contrary, readers will appreciate your fairness.

- *Have you used transitions to signal the sequence and relative importance of events?* Transitions between sentences can help you pinpoint causes or effects (*for this reason, as a result*), show the steps in a sequence (*first, second, third*), link events in time (*in the same month*), specify duration (*a year later*), and indicate the weights you assign events (*equally important, even more crucial*).

MALCOLM GLADWELL [b. 1963]

The Tipping Point

Born in England in 1963 to an English father and a West Indian mother, **Malcolm Gladwell** immigrated with his parents to Canada as a child. Gladwell received his bachelor's degree in history from the University of Toronto, after which he began his writing career at the *American Spectator.* He subsequently served with the *Washington Post,* first as a business and science reporter and later as chief of the *Post's* New York City bureau. While working as a staff writer for the *New Yorker,* where he has spent more than fifteen years, Gladwell became known for his highly readable articles that synthesize complex research in the sciences and social sciences. He has won numerous awards, including a National Magazine Award for his 1999 profile of Ron Popeil, and in 2005, he was named among the top one hundred most influential people in the world by *Time.* His books include *Blink: The Power of Thinking without Thinking* (2005) and *Outliers: The Story of Success* (2008). His latest work, *What the Dog Saw: And Other Adventures* (2009), is a compilation of his contributions to the *New Yorker.*

Gladwell's best-selling book *The Tipping Point: How Little Things Can Make a Big Difference,* an examination of why change occurs, was published in 2000. The title of the book—and of this excerpt—comes from epidemiology. As Gladwell defined it in an interview, the tipping point is "the name given to that moment in an epidemic when a virus reaches critical mass." Here, Gladwell focuses on the dramatic decrease in New York City's violent crime rate during the 1990s. The decrease, as he explains, was fueled in large part by strict policing of more minor crimes.

During the 1990s violent crime declined across the United States for a number of fairly straightforward reasons. The illegal trade in crack cocaine, which had spawned a great deal of violence among gangs and drug dealers, began to decline. The economy's dramatic recovery meant that many people who might have been lured into crime got legitimate

Malcolm Gladwell, "The Tipping Point." From *The Tipping Point: How Little Things Can Make a Big Difference* by Malcolm Gladwell. Copyright © 2000 by Malcolm Gladwell. Reprinted by permission of Little, Brown and Company, Inc.

jobs instead, and the general aging of the population meant that there were fewer people in the age range—males between eighteen and twenty-four—that is responsible for the majority of all violence. The question of why crime declined in New York City, however, is a little more complicated. In the period when the New York epidemic tipped down, the city's economy hadn't improved. It was still stagnant. In fact, the city's poorest neighborhoods had just been hit hard by the welfare cuts of the early 1990s. The waning of the crack cocaine epidemic in New York was clearly a factor, but then again, it had been in steady decline well before crime dipped. As for the aging of the population, because of heavy immigration to New York in the 1980s, the city was getting younger in the 1990s, not older. In any case, all of these trends are long-term changes that one would expect to have gradual effects. In New York the decline was anything but gradual. Something else clearly played a role in reversing New York's crime epidemic.

The most intriguing candidate for that "something else" is called the Broken Windows theory. Broken Windows was the brainchild of the criminologists James Q. Wilson and George Kelling. Wilson and Kelling argued that crime is the inevitable result of disorder. If a window is broken and left unrepaired, people walking by will conclude that no one cares and no one is in charge. Soon, more windows will be broken, and the sense of anarchy will spread from the building to the street on which it faces, sending a signal that anything goes. In a city, relatively minor problems like graffiti, public disorder, and aggressive panhandling, they write, are all the equivalent of broken windows, invitations to more serious crimes:

> Muggers and robbers, whether opportunistic or professional, believe they reduce their chances of being caught or even identified if they operate on streets where potential victims are already intimidated by prevailing conditions. If the neighborhood cannot keep a bothersome panhandler from annoying passersby, the thief may reason, it is even less likely to call the police to identify a potential mugger or to interfere if the mugging actually takes place.

This is an epidemic theory of crime. It says that crime is contagious— just as a fashion trend is contagious—that it can start with a broken window and spread to an entire community. The Tipping Point in this epidemic, though, isn't a particular kind of person—a Connector like Lois Weisberg or a Maven like Mark Alpert.[1] It's something physical like graffiti. The impetus to engage in a certain kind of behavior is not coming from a certain kind of person but from a feature of the environment.

In the mid-1980s Kelling was hired by the New York Transit Authority as a consultant, and he urged them to put the Broken Windows theory into practice. They obliged, bringing in a new subway director by the name of David Gunn to oversee a multibillion-dollar rebuilding of the subway system. Many subway advocates, at the time, told Gunn not to worry about graffiti, to focus on the larger questions of crime and subway reliability, and it seemed like reasonable advice. Worrying about graffiti at a time when the entire system was close to collapse seems as pointless as scrubbing the decks of the *Titanic* as it headed toward the icebergs. But Gunn insisted. "The graffiti was symbolic of the collapse of the system," he says. "When you looked at the process of rebuilding the organization and morale, you had to win the battle against graffiti. Without winning that battle, all the management reforms and physical changes just weren't going to happen. We were about to put out new trains that were worth about ten million bucks apiece, and unless we did something to protect them, we knew just what would happen. They would last one day and then they would be vandalized."

Gunn drew up a new management structure and a precise set of goals and timetables aimed at cleaning the system line by line, train by train. He started with the number seven train that connects Queens to midtown Manhattan, and began experimenting with new techniques to clean off the paint. On stainless-steel cars, solvents were used. On the painted cars, the graffiti were simply painted over. Gunn made it a rule that there should be no retreat, that once a car was "reclaimed" it should never be allowed to be vandalized again. "We were religious about it," Gunn said. At the end of the number one line in the Bronx, where the trains stop before turning around and going back to Manhattan, Gunn set up a cleaning station. If a car came in with graffiti, the graffiti had to be removed during the changeover, or the car was removed from service. "Dirty" cars, which hadn't yet been cleansed of graffiti, were never to be mixed with "clean" cars. The idea was to send an unambiguous message to the vandals themselves.

[1]In an earlier chapter of *The Tipping Point*, Gladwell discusses personality types who trigger major changes in society. Connectors have unusually large social circles, and Mavens are particularly knowledgeable about products, services, and prices. Lois Weisberg and Mark Alpert are two typical Americans whom Gladwell interviewed to illustrate these types.

"We had a yard up in Harlem on One hundred thirty-fifth Street where the trains would lay up over night," Gunn said. "The kids would come the first night and paint the side of the train white. Then they would come the next night, after it was dry, and draw the outline. Then they would come the third night and color it in. It was a three-day job. We knew the kids would be working on one of the dirty trains, and what we would do is wait for them to finish their mural. Then we'd walk over with rollers and paint it over. The kids would be in tears, but we'd just be going up and down, up and down. It was a message to them. If you want to spend three nights of your time vandalizing a train, fine. But it's never going to see the light of day."

Gunn's graffiti cleanup took from 1984 to 1990. At that point, the Transit Authority hired William Bratton to head the transit police, and the second stage of the reclamation of the subway system began. Bratton was, like Gunn, a disciple of Broken Windows. He describes Kelling, in fact, as his intellectual mentor, and so his first step as police chief was as seemingly quixotic as Gunn's. With felonies—serious crimes—on the subway system at an all-time high, Bratton decided to crack down on fare-beating. Why? Because he believed that, like graffiti, fare-beating could be a signal, a small expression of disorder that invited much more serious crimes. An estimated 170,000 people a day were entering the system, by one route or another, without paying a token. Some were kids, who simply jumped over the turnstiles. Others would lean backward on the turnstiles and force their way through. And once one or two or three people began cheating the system, other people—who might never otherwise have considered evading the law—would join in, reasoning that if some people weren't going to pay, they shouldn't either, and the problem would snowball. The problem was exacerbated by the fact fare-beating was not easy to fight. Because there was only $1.25 at stake, the transit police didn't feel it was worth their time to pursue it, particularly when there were plenty of more serious crimes happening down on the platform and in the trains.

Bratton is a colorful, charismatic man, a born leader, and he quickly made his presence felt. His wife stayed behind in Boston, so he was free to work long hours, and he would roam the city on the subway at night, getting a sense of what the problems were and how best to fight them. First, he picked stations where fare-beating was the biggest problem, and put as many as ten policemen in plainclothes at the turnstiles. The team would nab fare-beaters one by one, handcuff them, and leave them standing, in a daisy chain, on the platform until they had a "full catch." The idea was to signal, as publicly as possible, that the transit police were now serious about cracking down on fare-beaters. Previously, police officers had been wary of pursuing fare-beaters because the arrest, the trip to the station house, the filling out of necessary forms, and the waiting for those forms to be processed took an entire day—all for a crime that usually merited no more than a slap on the wrist. Bratton retrofitted a city bus and turned it into a rolling station house, with its own fax machines, phones, holding pen, and fingerprinting facilities. Soon the turnaround time on an arrest was down to an hour. Bratton also insisted that a check be run on all those arrested. Sure enough, one out of seven arrestees had an outstanding warrant for a previous crime, and one out of twenty was carrying a weapon of some sort. Suddenly it wasn't hard to convince police officers that tackling fare-beating made sense. "For the cops it was a bonanza," Bratton writes. "Every arrest was like opening a box of Cracker Jack. What kind of toy am I going to get? Got a gun? Got a knife? Got a warrant? Do we have a murderer here? . . . After a while the bad guys wised up and began to leave their weapons home and pay their fares." Under Bratton, the number of ejections from subway stations—for drunkenness, or improper behavior—tripled within his first few months in office. Arrests for misdemeanors, for the kind of minor offenses that had gone unnoticed in the past, went up five-fold between 1990 and 1994. Bratton turned the transit police into an organization focused on the smallest infractions, on the details of life underground.

After the election of Rudolph Giuliani as mayor of New York in 1994, Bratton was appointed head of the New York City Police Department, and he applied the same strategies to the city at large. He instructed his officers to crack down on quality-of-life crimes: on the "squeegee men" who came up to drivers at New York City intersections and demanded money for washing car windows, for example, and on all the other above-ground equivalents of turnstile-jumping and graffiti. "Previous police administration had been handcuffed by restrictions," Bratton says. "We took the handcuffs off. We stepped up enforcement of the laws against public drunkenness and public urination and arrested repeat violators, including those who threw empty bottles on the street or were involved in even relatively minor damage to property. . . . If you peed in the street, you were going to jail." When crime began to fall in the city—as quickly and dramatically as it had in the subways—Bratton and Giuliani pointed to the same cause. Minor, seemingly insignificant quality-of-life crimes, they said, were Tipping Points for violent crime.

[2000]

JOHN CIARDI [1916–1986]

Is Everybody Happy?

John Ciardi was born in Boston, the child of Italian immigrants. He attended Bates College and Tufts University and received a master's degree from the University of Michigan. Ciardi is best known for *How Does a Poem Mean?*, a 1959 work which became a standard text in many classrooms. He also wrote a well-received critique of Dante's *The Divine Comedy*, served as a regular commentator on National Public Radio, and was an editor for the *Saturday Review* for many years. Ciardi initiated his teaching career at the University of Kansas City and, following a term in the military, accepted a teaching post at Harvard University in 1946. In 1961, he relinquished his formal teaching duties to focus on his own literary work, though he remained active within the academic community through lectures, readings, and appearances on educational television. Ciardi sought to make his work accessible to mass audiences, but without sacrificing complexity or formal poetics. As a result, he eschewed "elevated" themes and poetic trends, writing in a style that gained him a large following. A recipient of the Prix de Rome, Ciardi published four volumes of poetry, including *Live another Day* (1949) and *The Birds of Pompeii* (1956).

The right to pursue happiness is issued to Americans with their birth certificates, but no one seems quite sure which way it ran. It may be we are issued a hunting license but offered no game. Jonathan Swift seemed to think so when he attacked the idea of happiness as "the possession of being well-deceived," the felicity of being "a fool among knaves." For Swift saw society as Vanity Fair, the land of false goals.

It is, of course, un-American to think in terms of fools and knaves. We do, however, seem to be dedicated to the idea of buying our way to happiness. We shall all have made it to Heaven when we possess enough.

And at the same time the forces of American commercialism are hugely dedicated to making us deliberately unhappy. Advertising is one of our major industries, and advertising exists not to satisfy desires but to create them—and to create them faster than any man's budget can satisfy them. For that matter, our whole economy is based on a dedicated insatiability.

John Ciardi, "Is Everybody Happy? " from *The Saturday Review*, March 14, 1964. By permission of the Ciardi Family Publishing Trust, John L. Ciardi, Trustee.

We are taught that to possess is to be happy, and then we are made to want. We are even told it is our duty to want. It was only a few years ago, to cite a single example, that car dealers across the country were flying banners that read "You Auto Buy Now." They were calling upon Americans, as an act approaching patriotism, to buy at once, with money they did not have, automobiles they did not really need, and which they would be required to grow tired of by the time the next year's models were released.

Or look at any of the women's magazines. There, as Bernard DeVoto once pointed out, advertising begins as poetry in the front pages and ends as pharmacopoeia and therapy in the back pages. The poetry of the front matter is the dream of perfect beauty. This is the baby skin that must be hers. These, the flawless teeth. This, the perfumed breath she must exhale. This, the sixteen-year-old figure she must display at forty, at fifty, at sixty, and forever.

Once past the vaguely uplifting fiction and feature articles, the reader 5 finds the other face of the dream in the back matter. This is the harness into which Mother must strap herself in order to display that perfect figure. These, the chin straps she must sleep in. This is the salve that restores all, this is her laxative, these are the tablets that melt away fat, these are the hormones of perpetual youth, these are the stockings that hide varicose veins.

Obviously no half-sane person can be completely persuaded either by such poetry or by such pharmacopoeia and orthopedics. Yet someone is obviously trying to buy the dream as offered and spending billions every year in the attempt. Clearly the happiness market is not running out of customers, but what are we trying to buy?

The idea "happiness," to be sure, will not sit still for easy definition: the best one can do is to try to set some extremes to the idea and then work in toward the middle. To think of happiness as acquisitive and competitive will do to set the materialistic extreme. To think of it as the idea one senses in, say, a holy man of India will do to set the spiritual extreme. That holy man's ideal of happiness is in needing nothing from outside himself. In wanting nothing, he lacks nothing. He sits immobile, rapt in contemplation, free even of his own body. Or nearly free of it. If devout admirers bring him food he eats it; if not, he starves indifferently. Why be concerned? What is physical is an illusion to him. Contemplation is his joy and he achieves it through a fantastically demanding discipline, the accomplishment of which is itself a joy within him.

Is he a happy man? Perhaps his happiness is only another sort of illusion. But who can take it from him? And who will dare say it is more illusory than happiness on the installment plan?

But, perhaps because I am Western, I doubt such catatonic happiness, as I doubt the dreams of the happiness market. What is certain is that his way of happiness would be torture to almost any Western man. Yet these extremes will still serve to frame the area within which all of us must find some sort of balance. Thoreau—a creature of both Eastern and Western thought—had his own firm sense of that balance. His aim was to save on the low levels in order to spend on the high.

Possession for its own sake or in competition with the rest of the 10 neighborhood would have been Thoreau's idea of the low levels. The active discipline of heightening one's perception of what is enduring in nature would have been his idea of the high. What he saved from the low was time and effort he could spend on the high. Thoreau certainly disapproved of starvation, but he would put into feeding himself only as much effort as would keep him functioning for more important efforts.

Effort is the gist of it. There is no happiness except as we take on life-engaging difficulties. Short of the impossible, as Yeats put it, the satisfactions we get from a lifetime depend on how high we choose our difficulties. Robert Frost was thinking in something like the same terms when he spoke of "the pleasure of taking pains." The mortal flaw in the advertised version of happiness is in the fact that it purports to be effortless.

We demand difficulty even in our games. We demand it because without difficulty there can be no game. A game is a way of making something hard for the fun of it. The rules of the game are an arbitrary imposition of difficulty. When the spoilsport ruins the fun, he always does so by refusing to play by the rules. It is easier to win at chess if you are free, at your pleasure, to change the wholly arbitrary rules, but the fun is in winning within the rules. No difficulty, no fun.

The buyers and sellers at the happiness market seem too often to have lost their sense of the pleasure of difficulty. Heaven knows what they are playing, but it seems a dull game. The Indian holy man seems dull to us, I suppose, because he seems to be refusing to play anything at all. The Western weakness may be in the illusion that happiness can be bought. Perhaps the Eastern weakness is in the idea that there is such a thing as perfect (and therefore static) happiness.

Happiness is never more than partial. There are no pure states of mankind. Whatever else happiness may be, it is neither in having nor in being, but in becoming. What the Founding Fathers declared for us as an inherent right, we should do well to remember, was not happiness but the *pursuit* of happiness. What they might have underlined, could they have foreseen the happiness market, is the cardinal fact that happiness is in the pursuit itself, in the meaningful pursuit of what is life-engaging and life-revealing, which is to say, in the idea of *becoming*. A nation is not measured by what it possesses or wants to possess, but by what it wants to become.

By all means let the happiness market sell us minor satisfactions and 15
even minor follies so long as we keep them in scale and buy them out of
spiritual change. I am no customer for either puritanism or asceticism.
But drop any real spiritual capital at those bazaars, and what you come
home to will be your own poorhouse.

HENRY DAVID THOREAU [1817–1862]

Where I Lived, and What I Lived For

Henry David Thoreau was born in 1817 and raised in Concord, Massachusetts, living there for most of his life. Along with Ralph Waldo Emerson, Thoreau was one of the most important thinkers of his time in America and is still widely read today. *Walden* (1854), the work for which he is best known, is drawn from the journal he kept during his two-year-long stay in a cabin on Walden Pond. In *Walden*, Thoreau explores his interests in naturalism, individualism, and self-sufficiency. He is also remembered for his essay "Civil Disobedience" (1849), an early, influential statement of this tactic of protest later practiced by Mahatma Gandhi and, under the leadership of Martin Luther King Jr., many in the civil rights movement.

"Where I Lived, and What I Lived For" is taken from *Walden*. In it, Thoreau makes the argument for his going to live in the woods. Writing about *Walden*, scholars have pointed out that Thoreau was not particularly deep in the woods and that he was regularly visited and supplied with, among other things, pies. As you read, consider how this influences your acceptance of what he has to say.

I went to the woods because I wished to live deliberately, to front only the essential facts of life, and see if I could not learn what it had to teach, and not, when I came to die, discover that I had not lived. I did not wish to live what was not life, living is so dear; nor did I wish to practice resignation, unless it was quite necessary. I wanted to live deep and suck out all the marrow of life, to live so sturdily and Spartan-like as to put to rout all that was not life, to cut a broad swath and shave close, to drive life into a corner, and reduce it to its lowest terms, and, if it proved to be mean, why then to get the whole and genuine meanness of it, and publish its meanness to the world; or if it were sublime, to know it by experience, and be able to give a true account of it in my next excursion. For most men, it appears to me, are in a strange uncertainty about it, whether it is of the devil or of God, and have *somewhat hastily* concluded that it is the chief end of man here to "glorify God and enjoy him forever."

Still we live meanly, like ants; though the fable tells us that we were long ago changed into men; like pygmies we fight with cranes; it is error upon error, and clout upon clout, and our best virtue has for its occasion a superfluous and evitable wretchedness. Our life is frittered away by detail. An honest man has hardly need to count more than his ten fingers, or in extreme cases he may add his ten toes, and lump the rest. Simplicity, simplicity, simplicity! I say, let your affairs be as two or three, and not a hundred or a thousand; instead of a million count half a dozen, and keep your accounts on your thumb-nail. In the midst of this chopping sea of civilized life, such are the clouds and storms and quicksands and thousand-and-one items to be allowed for, that a man has to live, if he would not founder and go to the bottom and not make his port at all, by dead reckoning, and he must be a great calculator indeed who succeeds. Simplify, simplify. Instead of three meals a day, if it be necessary eat but one; instead of a hundred dishes, five; and reduce other things in proportion. Our life is like a German Confederacy, made of up petty states, with its boundary forever fluctuating, so that even a German cannot tell you how it is bounded at any moment. The nation itself, with all its so-called internal improvements, which, by the way are all external and superficial, is just such an unwieldy and overgrown establishment, cluttered with furniture and tripped up by its own traps, ruined by luxury and heedless expense, by want of calculation and a worthy aim, as the million households in the lands; and the only cure for it, as for them, is in a rigid economy, a stern and more than Spartan simplicity of life and elevation of purpose. It lives too fast. Men think that it is essential that the *Nation* have commerce, and export ice, and talk through a telegraph, and ride thirty miles an hour, without a doubt, whether *they* do or not; but whether we should live like baboons or like men, is a little uncertain. If we do not get our sleepers, and forge rails, and devote days and nights to the work, but go to tinkering upon our *lives* to improve *them*, who will build railroads? And if railroads are not built, how shall we get to heaven in season? But if we stay at home and mind our business, who will want railroads? We do not ride on the railroad; it rides upon us. Did you ever think what those sleepers are that underlie the railroad? Each one is a man, an Irishman, or a Yankee man. The rails are laid on them, and they are covered with sand, and the cars run smoothly over them. They are sound sleepers, I assure you. And every few years a new lot is laid down and run over, so that, if some have the pleasure of riding on a rail, others have the misfortune to be ridden upon. And when they run over a man that is walking in his sleep, a supernumerary sleeper in the wrong position, and wake him up, they suddenly stop the cars, and make a hue and cry about it, as if this were an exception. I am glad to know that it takes a gang of men for every five miles to keep the sleepers down and level in their beds as it is, for this is a sign that they may sometimes get up again.

Why should we live with such hurry and waste of life? We are determined to be starved before we are hungry. Men say that a stitch in time saves nine, and so they take a thousand stitches to-day to save nine to-morrow. As for *work*, we haven't any of any consequence. We have the Saint Vitus' dance, and cannot possibly keep our heads still. If I should only give a few pulls at the parish bell-rope, as for a fire, that is, without setting the bell, there is hardly a man on his farm in the outskirts of Concord, notwithstanding that press of engagements which was his excuse so many times this morning, nor a boy, nor a woman, I might almost say, but would foresake all and follow that sound, not mainly to save property from the flames, but, if we will confess the truth, much more to see it burn, since burn it must, and we, be it known, did not set it on fire—or to see it put out, and have a hand in it, if that is done as handsomely; yes, even if it were the parish church itself. Hardly a man takes a half-hour's nap after dinner, but when he wakes he holds up his head and asks, "What's the news?" as if the rest of mankind had stood his sentinels. Some give directions to be waked every half-hour, doubtless for no other purpose; and then, to pay for it, they tell what they have dreamed. After a night's sleep the news is as indispensable as the breakfast. "Pray tell me anything new that has happened to a man anywhere on this globe"—and he reads it over his coffee and rolls, that a man has had his eyes gouged out this morning on the Wachito River; never dreaming the while that he lives in the dark unfathomed mammoth cave of this world, and has but the rudiment of an eye himself.

For my part, I could easily do without the post-office. I think that there are very few important communications made through it. To speak critically, I never received more than one or two letters in my life—I wrote this some years ago—that were worth the postage. The penny-post is, commonly, an institution through which you seriously offer a man that penny for his thoughts which is so often safely offered in jest. And I am sure that I never read any memorable news in a newspaper. If we read of one man robbed, or murdered, or killed by accident, or one house burned, or one vessel wrecked or one steamboat blown up, or one cow run over on the Western Railroad, or one mad dog killed, or one lot of grasshoppers in the winter—we never need read of another. One is enough. If you are acquainted with the principle, what do you care for a myriad instances and applications? To a philosopher all *news*, as it is called, is gossip, and they who edit and read it are old women over their tea. Yet not a few are greedy after this gossip. There was such a rush, as I hear, the other day at one of the offices to learn the foreign news by the last arrival, that several large squares of plate glass belonging to the establishment were broken by the pressure—news which I seriously think a ready wit might write a twelvemonth, or twelve years, beforehand with sufficient accuracy. As for Spain, for instance, if you know how to throw in Don Carlos and the Infanta, and Don Pedro and Seville and Granada, from time to time in the right proportions—they may have changed the names a little since I saw the papers—and serve up a bullfight when other entertainments fail, it will be true to the letter, and give us as good an idea of the exact state or ruin of things in Spain as the most succinct and lucid reports under this head in the newspapers; and as for England, almost the last significant scrap of news from that quarter was the revolution of 1649; and if you have learned the history of her crops for an average year, you never need attend to that thing again, unless your speculations are of a merely pecuniary character. If one may judge who rarely looks into the newspapers, nothing new does ever happen in foreign parts, a French revolution not excepted.

What news! how much more important to know what that is which   5
was never old! "Kieou-he-yu (great dignitary of the state of Wei) sent a man to Khoung-tseu to know his news. Khoung-tseu caused the messenger to be seated near him, and questioned him in these terms: What is your master doing? The messenger answered with respect: My master desires to diminish the number of his faults, but he cannot come to the end of them. The messenger being gone, the philosopher remarked: What a worthy messenger! What a worthy messenger!" The preacher, instead of vexing the ears of drowsy farmers on their day of rest at the end of the week—for Sunday is the fit conclusion of an ill-spent week, and not the fresh and brave beginning of a new one—with this one other draggle-tail of a sermon, should shout with thundering voice, "Pause! Avast! Why so seeming fast, but deadly slow?"

Shams and delusions are esteemed for soundest truths, while reality is fabulous. If men would steadily observe realities only, and not allow themselves to be deluded, life, to compare it with such things as we know, would be like a fairy tale and the Arabian Nights' Entertainments. If we respected only what is inevitable and has a right to be, music and poetry would resound along the streets. When we are unhurried and wise, we perceive that only great and worthy things have any permanent and absolute existence, that petty fears and petty pleasures are but the shadow of the reality. This is always exhilarating and sublime. By closing the eyes and slumbering, and consenting to be deceived by shows, men establish and confirm their daily life of routine and habit everywhere, which still is built on purely illusory foundations. Children, who play life, discern its true law and relations more clearly than men, who fail to live it worthily, but who think that they are wiser by experience, that is, by failure. I have read in a Hindoo book, that "there was a king's son, who, being expelled in infancy from his native city, was brought up by a forester, and, growing up to maturity in that state, imagined himself to belong to the barbarous race with which he lived. One of his father's ministers having discovered him, revealed to him what he was, and the misconception of his character was removed, and he knew himself to be a prince. So soul," continues the Hindoo philosopher, "from the circumstances in which it is placed, mistakes its own character, until the truth is revealed to it by some holy teacher and then it knows itself to be *Brahme*." I perceive that we inhabitants of New England live this mean life that we do because our vision does not penetrate the surface of things. We think that that *is* which *appears* to be. If a man should walk through this town and see only the reality, where, think you, would the "Milldam" go to? If he should give us an account of the realities he beheld there, we should not recognize the place in his description. Look at the meetinghouse, or a courthouse, or a jail, or a shop, or a dwelling-house, and say what that thing really is before a true gaze, and they would all go to pieces in your account of them. Men esteem truth remote, in the outskirts of the system, behind the farthest star, before Adam and after the last man. In eternity there is indeed something true and sublime. But all these times and places and occasions are now and here. God himself culminates in the present moment, and will never be more divine in the lapse of all the ages. And we are enabled to apprehend at all what is sublime and noble only by the perpetual instilling and drenching of the reality that surrounds us. The universe constantly and obediently answers to our conceptions; whether we travel fast or slow, the track is laid for us. Let us spend our lives in conceiving then. The poet or the artist never yet had so fair and noble a design but some of his posterity at least could accomplish it.

Let us spend one day as deliberately as Nature, and not be thrown off the track by every nutshell and mosquito's wing that falls on the rails. Let us rise early and fast, or breakfast, gently and without perturbation; let company come and let company go, let the bells ring and the children cry—determined to make a day of it. Why should we knock under and go with the stream? Let us not be upset and overwhelmed in that terrible rapid and whirlpool called a dinner, situated in the meridian shallows. Weather this danger and you are safe, for the rest of the way is downhill. With unrelaxed nerves, with morning vigor, sail by it, looking another way, tied to the mast like Ulysses. If the engine whistles, let it whistle till it is hoarse for its pains. If the bell rings, why should we run? We will consider what kind of music they are like. Let us settle ourselves and work and wedge our feet downward through the mud and slush of opinion, and prejudice, and tradition, and delusion, and appearance, that alluvion which covers the globe, through Paris and London, through New

York and Boston and Concord, through Church and State, through poetry and philosophy and religion, till we come to a hard bottom and rocks in place, which we can call *reality*, and say, This is, and no mistake; and then begin, having a *point d'appui*, below freshet and frost and fire, a place where you might found a wall or a state, or set a lamppost safely, or perhaps a gauge, not a Nilometer, but a Realometer, that future ages might know how deep a freshet of shams and appearances had gathered from time to time. If you stand right fronting and face to face to a fact, you will see the sun glimmer on both its surfaces, as if it were a cimeter, and feel its sweet edge dividing you through the heart and marrow, and so you will happily conclude your mortal career. Be it life or death, we crave only reality. If we are really dying, let us hear the rattle in our throats and feel cold in the extremities; if we are alive, let us go about our business.

Time is but the stream I go afishing in. I drink at it; but while I drink I see the sandy bottom and detect how shallow it is. Its thin current slides away but eternity remains. I would drink deeper; fish in the sky, whose bottom is pebbly with stars. I cannot count one. I know not the first letter of the alphabet. I have always been regretting that I was not as wise as the day I was born. The intellect is a cleaver; it discerns and rifts its way into the secret of things. I do not wish to be any more busy with my hands than is necessary. My head is hands and feet. I feel all my best faculties concentrated in it. My instinct tells me that my head is an organ for burrowing, as some creatures use their snout and fore paws, and with it I would mine and burrow my way through these hills. I think that the richest vein is somewhere hereabouts; so by the divining-rod and thin rising vapors, I judge; and here I will begin to mine.

[1854]

102

ERNEST HEMINGWAY [1899–1961]

Hills Like White Elephants

Born in Oak Park, Illinois, **Ernest Hemingway** (1899–1961) led an active, vigorous life from childhood, summering in the wilds of northern Michigan with his physician father and boxing and playing football at school. His first job as a writer was as a reporter for the Kansas City *Star.* During World War I he served as an ambulance driver in Italy; severely wounded before he had turned nineteen, he was decorated by the Italian government. Later, while working in Paris as a correspondent for the Toronto *Star,* he met Gertrude Stein, Ezra Pound, F. Scott Fitzgerald, and other artists and writers who had a significant influence on his work. Hemingway's first book, *Three Stories and Ten Poems* (1923), was followed by the well-known story collection *In Our Time* (1924; rev. and enl. ed., 1925). His novel *The Sun Also Rises* (1926) brought acclaim as well as recognition of Hemingway as the spokesman for the "lost generation." *A Farewell to Arms* (1929), based on his wartime experiences in Italy, and *For Whom the Bell Tolls* (1940), drawn from his time as a correspondent during the civil war in Spain, established his enduring reputation. In World War II he served as a correspondent and received a Bronze Star. His frequent travels took him to Spain for the bullfights, on fishing trips to the Caribbean, and on big-game expeditions to the American West and to Africa. In his later years he suffered from declining physical health and severe depression, which led to his suicide at his home in Ketcham, Idaho. The fullest collection of his short stories, the Finca-Vigia edition, came out in 1991. Hemingway was awarded the Nobel Prize in literature in 1954.

The hills across the valley of the Ebro were long and white. On this side there was no shade and no trees and the station was between two lines of rails in the sun. Close against the side of the station there was the warm shadow of the building and a curtain, made of strings of bamboo beads, hung across the open door into the bar, to keep out flies. The American and the girl with him sat at a table in the shade, outside the building. It

"Hills Like White Elephants." From *Men Without Women* by Ernest Hemingway. Copyright © 1927 by Charles Scribner's Sons. Copyright renewed 1955 by Ernest Hemingway. Reprinted with permission of Scribner, an imprint of Simon & Schuster Adult Publishing Group.

was very hot and the express from Barcelona would come in forty minutes. It stopped at this junction for two minutes and went on to Madrid.

"What should we drink?" the girl asked. She had taken off her hat and put it on the table.

"It's pretty hot," the man said.

"Let's drink beer."

"*Dos cervezas,*" the man said into the curtain.

"Big ones?" a woman asked from the doorway.

"Yes. Two big ones."

The woman brought two glasses of beer and two felt pads. She put the felt pads and the beer glasses on the table and looked at the man and the girl. The girl was looking off at the line of hills. They were white in the sun and the country was brown and dry.

"They look like white elephants," she said.

"I've never seen one," the man drank his beer.

"No, you wouldn't have."

"I might have," the man said. "Just because you say I wouldn't have doesn't prove anything."

The girl looked at the bead curtain. "They've painted something on it," she said. "What does it say?"

"Anis del Toro. It's a drink."

"Could we try it?"

The man called "Listen" through the curtain. The woman came out from the bar.

"Four reales."°

"We want two Anis del Toro."

"With water?"

"Do you want it with water?"

"I don't know," the girl said. "Is it good with water?"

"It's all right."

"You want them with water?" asked the woman.

"Yes, with water."

"It tastes like licorice," the girl said and put the glass down.

"That's the way with everything."

"Yes," said the girl. "Everything tastes of licorice. Especially all the things you've waited so long for, like absinthe."

"Oh, cut it out."

"You started it," the girl said. "I was being amused. I was having a fine time."

"Well, let's try and have a fine time."

Reales: Spanish silver coins.

"All right. I was trying. I said the mountains looked like white elephants. Wasn't that bright?"

"That was bright."

"I wanted to try this new drink: That's all we do, isn't it—look at things and try new drinks?"

"I guess so."

The girl looked across at the hills.

"They're lovely hills," she said. "They don't really look like white elephants. I just meant the coloring of their skin through the trees."

"Should we have another drink?"

"All right."

The warm wind blew the bead curtain against the table.

"The beer's nice and cool," the man said.

"It's lovely," the girl said.

"It's really an awfully simple operation, Jig," the man said. "It's not really an operation at all."

The girl looked at the ground the table legs rested on.

"I know you wouldn't mind it, Jig. It's really not anything. It's just to let the air in."

The girl did not say anything.

"I'll go with you and I'll stay with you all the time. They just let the air in and then it's all perfectly natural."

"Then what will we do afterward?"

"We'll be fine afterward. Just like we were before."

"What makes you think so?"

"That's the only thing that bothers us. It's the only thing that's made us unhappy."

The girl looked at the bead curtain, put her hand out, and took hold of two of the strings of beads.

"And you think then we'll be all right and be happy."

"I know we will. You don't have to be afraid. I've known lots of people that have done it."

"So have I," said the girl. "And afterward they were all so happy."

"Well," the man said, "if you don't want to you don't have to. I wouldn't have you do it if you didn't want to. But I know it's perfectly simple."

"And you really want to?"

"I think it's the best thing to do. But I don't want you to do it if you don't really want to."

"And if I do it you'll be happy and things will be like they were and you'll love me?"

"I love you now. You know I love you."

"I know. But if I do it, then it will be nice again if I say things are like white elephants, and you'll like it?"

"I'll love it. I love it now but I just can't think about it. You know how I get when I worry."

"If I do it you won't ever worry?"

"I won't worry about that because it's perfectly simple."

"Then I'll do it. Because I don't care about me."

"What do you mean?"

"I don't care about me."

"Well, I care about you."

"Oh, yes. But I don't care about me. And I'll do it and then everything will be fine."

"I don't want you to do it if you feel that way."

The girl stood up and walked to the end of the station. Across, on the other side, were fields of grain and trees along the banks of the Ebro. Far away, beyond the river, were mountains. The shadow of a cloud moved across the field of grain and she saw the river through the trees.

"And we could have all this," she said. "And we could have everything and every day we make it more impossible."

"What did you say?"

"I said we could have everything."

"We can have everything."

"No, we can't."

"We can have the whole world."

"No, we can't."

"We can go everywhere."

"No, we can't. It isn't ours any more."

"It's ours."

"No, it isn't. And once they take it away, you never get it back."

"But they haven't taken it away."

"We'll wait and see."

"Come on back in the shade," he said. "You mustn't feel that way."

"I don't feel any way," the girl said. "I just know things."

"I don't want you to do anything that you don't want to do——"

"Nor that isn't good for me," she said. "I know. Could we have another beer?"

"All right. But you've got to realize——"

"I realize," the girl said. "Can't we maybe stop talking?"

They sat down at the table and the girl looked across at the hills on the dry side of the valley and the man looked at her and at the table.

"You've got to realize," he said, "that I don't want you to do it if you don't want to. I'm perfectly willing to go through with it if it means anything to you."

"Doesn't it mean anything to you? We could get along."

"Of course it does. But I don't want anybody but you. I don't want any one else. And I know it's perfectly simple."

"Yes, you know it's perfectly simple."

"It's all right for you to say that, but I do know it."

"Would you do something for me now?"

"I'd do anything for you."

"Would you please please please please please please please stop talking?"

He did not say anything but looked at the bags against the wall of the station. There were labels on them from all the hotels where they had spent nights.

"But I don't want you to," he said, "I don't care anything about it."

"I'll scream," the girl said.

The woman came out through the curtains with two glasses of beer and put them down on the damp felt pads. "The train comes in five minutes," she said.

"What did she say?" asked the girl.

"That the train is coming in five minutes."

The girl smiled brightly at the woman, to thank her.

"I'd better take the bags over to the other side of the station," the man said. She smiled at him.

"All right. Then come back and we'll finish the beer."

He picked up the two heavy bags and carried them around the station to the other tracks. He looked up the tracks but could not see the train. Coming back, he walked through the barroom, where people waiting for the train were drinking. He drank an Anis at the bar and looked at the people. They were all waiting reasonably for the train. He went out through the bead curtain. She was sitting at the table and smiled at him.

"Do you feel better?" he asked.

"I feel fine," she said. "There's nothing wrong with me. I feel fine."

[1927]

107

NATHANIEL HAWTHORNE [1804–1864]

Young Goodman Brown

Born in Salem, Massachusetts, into a family descended from the New England Puritans, **Nathaniel Hawthorne** (1804–1864) graduated from Bowdoin College, Maine, in 1825. For the next twelve years he lived in Salem in relative seclusion, reading, observing the New England landscape and people, and writing his first novel, *Fanshawe* (published anonymously in 1828), and the first series of *Twice-Told Tales* (1837). (The second series, published in 1842, was reviewed by Edgar Allan Poe and won some notice.) To support himself Hawthorne took a job in the Boston customhouse, resigning in 1841 to live at Brook Farm, a utopian community. The following year he left Brook Farm, married Sophia Peabody, and moved to Concord, Massachusetts, where his neighbors included Ralph Waldo Emerson and Henry David Thoreau. There he wrote the stories collected in *Mosses from an Old Manse* (1846). Returning to Salem, he took a position as a customs inspector and began full-time work on what was to become his most celebrated novel, *The Scarlet Letter* (1850). The novels *The House of the Seven Gables* (1851) and *The Blithedale Romance* (1852), based on his Brook Farm experience, quickly followed. Also in 1852, he wrote a campaign biography of Franklin Pierce, a former college friend who, on becoming president, appointed Hawthorne U.S. consul at Liverpool. Hawthorne's subsequent travels in Europe contributed to the novel *The Marble Faun* (1860), his last major work.

Young Goodman Brown came forth at sunset into the street at Salem village; but put his head back, after crossing the threshold, to exchange a parting kiss with his young wife. And Faith, as the wife was aptly named, thrust her own pretty head into the street, letting the wind play with the pink ribbons of her cap while she called to Goodman Brown.

"Dearest heart," whispered she, softly and rather sadly, when her lips were close to his ear, "prithee put off your journey until sunrise and sleep in your own bed to-night. A lone woman is troubled with such dreams and such thoughts that she's afeared of herself sometimes. Pray tarry with me this night, dear husband, of all nights in the year."

"My love and my Faith," replied young Goodman Brown, "of all nights in the year, this one night must I tarry away from thee. My journey, as thou callest it, forth and back again, must needs be done 'twixt now and sunrise. What, my sweet, pretty wife, dost thou doubt me already, and we but three months married?"

"Then God bless you!" said Faith, with the pink ribbons, "and may you find all well when you come back."

"Amen!" cried Goodman Brown. "Say thy prayers, dear Faith, and go to bed at dusk, and no harm will come to thee."

So they parted; and the young man pursued his way until, being about to turn the corner by the meeting-house, he looked back and saw the head of Faith still peeping after him with a melancholy air, in spite of her pink ribbons.

"Poor little Faith!" thought he, for his heart smote him. "What a wretch am I to leave her on such an errand! She talks of dreams, too. Methought as she spoke there was trouble in her face, as if a dream had warned her what work is to be done to-night. But no, no; 't would kill her to think it. Well, she's a blessed angel on earth, and after this one night I'll cling to her skirts and follow her to heaven."

With this excellent resolve for the future, Goodman Brown felt himself justified in making more haste on his present evil purpose. He had taken a dreary road, darkened by all the gloomiest trees of the forest, which barely stood aside to let the narrow path creep through, and closed immediately behind. It was all as lonely as could be; and there is this peculiarity in such a solitude, that the traveller knows not who may be concealed by the innumerable trunks and the thick boughs overhead; so that with lonely footsteps he may yet be passing through an unseen multitude.

"There may be a devilish Indian behind every tree," said Goodman Brown to himself; and he glanced fearfully behind him as he added, "What if the devil himself should be at my very elbow!"

His head being turned back, he passed a crook of the road, and, looking forward again, beheld the figure of a man, in grave and decent attire, seated at the foot of an old tree. He arose at Goodman Brown's approach and walked onward side by side with him.

"You are late, Goodman Brown," said he. "The clock of the Old South was striking as I came through Boston, and that is full fifteen minutes agone."

"Faith kept me back a while," replied the young man, with a tremor in his voice, caused by the sudden appearance of his companion, though not wholly unexpected.

It was now deep dusk in the forest, and deepest in that part of it where these two were journeying. As nearly as could be discerned, the second traveller was about fifty years old, apparently in the same rank of life as Goodman Brown, and bearing a considerable resemblance to him, though perhaps more in expression than features. Still they might have been taken for father and son. And yet, though the elder person was as simply clad as the younger, and as simple in manner too, he had an indescribable air of one who knew the world, and who would not have felt abashed at the governor's dinner table or in King William's court, were it possible that his affairs should call him thither. But the only thing about him that could be fixed upon as remarkable was his staff, which bore the likeness of a great black snake, so curiously wrought that it might almost be seen to twist and wriggle itself like a living serpent. This, of course, must have been an ocular deception, assisted by the uncertain light.

"Come, Goodman Brown," cried his fellow-traveller, "this is a dull pace for the beginning of a journey. Take my staff, if you are so soon weary."

"Friend," said the other, exchanging his slow pace for a full stop, "having kept covenant by meeting thee here, it is my purpose now to return whence I came. I have scruples touching the matter thou wot'st of."

"Sayest thou so?" replied he of the serpent, smiling apart. "Let us walk on, nevertheless, reasoning as we go; and if I convince thee not thou shalt turn back. We are but a little way in the forest yet."

"Too far! too far!" exclaimed the goodman, unconsciously resuming his walk. "My father never went into the woods on such an errand, nor his father before him. We have been a race of honest men and good Christians since the days of the martyrs; and shall I be the first of the name of Brown that ever took this path and kept"—

"Such company, thou wouldst say," observed the elder person, interpreting his pause. "Well said, Goodman Brown! I have been as well acquainted with your family as with ever a one among the Puritans; and that's no trifle to say. I helped your grandfather, the constable, when he lashed the Quaker woman so smartly through the streets of Salem; and it was I that brought your father a pitch-pine knot, kindled at my own hearth, to set fire to an Indian village, in King Philip's war.° They were my good friends, both; and many a pleasant walk have we had along this path, and returned merrily after midnight. I would fain be friends with you for their sake."

"If it be as thou sayest," replied Goodman Brown, "I marvel they never spoke of these matters; or, verily, I marvel not, seeing that the least rumor of the sort would have driven them from New England. We are a people of prayer, and good works to boot, and abide no such wickedness."

"Wickedness or not," said the traveller with the twisted staff, "I have a very general acquaintance here in New England. The deacons of many a

King Philip: Wampanoag chief who waged war against the New England colonists (1675–76).

church have drunk the communion wine with me; the selectmen of divers towns make me their chairman; and a majority of the Great and General Court are firm supporters of my interest. The governor and I, too — But these are state secrets."

"Can this be so?" cried Goodman Brown, with a stare of amazement at his undisturbed companion. "Howbeit, I have nothing to do with the governor and council; they have their own ways, and are no rule for a simple husbandman like me. But, were I to go on with thee, how should I meet the eye of that good old man, our minister, at Salem village? Oh, his voice would make me tremble both Sabbath day and lecture day."

Thus far the elder traveller had listened with due gravity; but now burst into a fit of irrepressible mirth, shaking himself so violently that his snake-like staff actually seemed to wriggle in sympathy.

"Ha! ha! ha!" shouted he again and again; then composing himself, "Well, go on, Goodman Brown, go on; but, prithee, don't kill me with laughing."

"Well, then, to end the matter at once," said Goodman Brown, considerably nettled, "there is my wife, Faith. It would break her dear little heart; and I'd rather break my own."

"Nay, if that be the case," answered the other, "e'en go thy ways, Goodman Brown. I would not for twenty old women like the one hobbling before us that Faith should come to any harm."

As he spoke he pointed his staff at a female figure on the path, in whom Goodman Brown recognized a very pious and exemplary dame, who had taught him his catechism in youth, and was still his moral and spiritual adviser, jointly with the minister and Deacon Gookin.

"A marvel, truly that Goody Cloyse should be so far in the wilderness at nightfall," said he. "But with your leave, friend, I shall take a cut through the woods until we have left this Christian woman behind. Being a stranger to you, she might ask whom I was consorting with and whither I was going."

"Be it so," said his fellow-traveller. "Betake you to the woods, and let me keep the path."

Accordingly the young man turned aside, but took care to watch his companion, who advanced softly along the road until he had come within a staff's length of the old dame. She, meanwhile, was making the best of her way, with singular speed for so aged a woman, and mumbling some indistinct words—a prayer, doubtless—as she went. The traveller put forth his staff and touched her withered neck with what seemed the serpent's tail.

"The devil!" screamed the pious old lady.

"Then Goody Cloyse knows her old friend?" observed the traveller, confronting her and leaning on his writhing stick.

"Ah, forsooth, and is it your worship indeed?" cried the good dame. "Yea, truly is it, and in the very image of my old gossip, Goodman Brown, the grandfather of the silly fellow that now is. But—would your worship believe it?—my broomstick hath strangely disappeared, stolen, as I suspect, by that unhanged witch, Goody Cory, and that, too, when I was all anointed with the juice of smallage, and cinquefoil, and wolf's bane"—

"Mingled with fine wheat and the fat of a new-born babe," said the shape of old Goodman Brown.

"Ah, your worship knows the recipe," cried the old lady, cackling aloud. "So, as I was saying, being all ready for the meeting, and no horse to ride on, I made up my mind to foot it; for they tell me there is a nice young man to be taken into communion to-night. But now your good worship will lend me your arm, and we shall be there in a twinkling."

"That can hardly be," answered her friend. "I may not spare you my arm, Goody Cloyse; but here is my staff, if you will."

So saying, he threw it down at her feet, where, perhaps, it assumed life, being one of the rods which its owner had formerly lent to the Egyptian magi. Of this fact, however, Goodman Brown could not take cognizance. He had cast up his eyes in astonishment, and, looking down again, beheld neither Goody Cloyse nor the serpentine staff, but his fellow-traveller alone, who waited for him as calmly as if nothing had happened.

"That old woman taught me my catechism," said the young man; and there was a world of meaning in this simple comment.

They continued to walk onward, while the elder traveller exhorted his companion to make good speed and persevere in the path, discoursing so aptly that his arguments seemed rather to spring up in the bosom of his auditor than to be suggested by himself. As they went, he plucked a branch of maple to serve for a walking stick, and began to strip it of the twigs and little boughs, which were wet with evening dew. The moment his fingers touched them they became strangely withered and dried up as with a week's sunshine. Thus the pair proceeded, at a good free pace, until suddenly, in a gloomy hollow of the road, Goodman Brown sat himself down on the stump of a tree and refused to go any farther.

"Friend," he said, stubbornly, "my mind is made up. Not another step will I budge on this errand. What if a wretched old woman do choose to go to the devil when I thought she was going to heaven: is that any reason why I should quit my dear Faith and go after her?"

"You will think better of this by and by," said his acquaintance, composedly. "Sit here and rest yourself a while; and when you feel like moving again, there is my staff to help you along."

Without more words, he threw his companion the maple stick, and was as speedily out of sight as if he had vanished into the deepening gloom. The young man sat a few moments by the roadside, applauding himself greatly, and thinking with how clear a conscience he should meet the minister in his morning walk, nor shrink from the eye of good old Deacon Gookin. And what calm sleep would be his that very night, which was to have been spent so wickedly, but so purely and sweetly now, in the arms of Faith! Amidst these pleasant and praiseworthy meditations, Goodman Brown heard the tramp of horses along the road, and deemed it advisable to conceal himself within the verge of the forest, conscious of the guilty purpose that had brought him thither, though now so happily turned from it.

On came the hoof tramps and the voices of the riders, two grave old voices, conversing soberly as they drew near. These mingled sounds appeared to pass along the road, within a few yards of the young man's hiding-place; but, owing doubtless to the depth of the gloom at that particular spot, neither the travellers nor their steeds were visible. Though their figures brushed the small boughs by the wayside, it could not be seen that they intercepted, even for a moment, the faint gleam from the strip of bright sky athwart which they must have passed. Goodman Brown alternately crouched and stood on tiptoe, pulling aside the branches and thrusting forth his head as far as he durst without discerning so much as a shadow. It vexed him the more, because he could have sworn, were such a thing possible, that he recognized the voices of the minister and Deacon Gookin, jogging along quietly, as they were wont to do, when bound to some ordination or ecclesiastical council. While yet within hearing, one of the riders stopped to pluck a switch.

"Of the two, reverend sir," said the voice like the deacon's, "I had rather miss an ordination dinner than to-night's meeting. They tell me that some of our community are to be here from Falmouth and beyond, and others from Connecticut and Rhode Island, besides several of the Indian powwows, who, after their fashion, know almost as much deviltry as the best of us. Moreover, there is a goodly young woman to be taken into communion."

"Mighty well, Deacon Gookin!" replied the solemn old tones of the minister. "Spur up, or we shall be late. Nothing can be done, you know, until I get on the ground."

The hoofs clattered again; and the voices, talking so strangely in the empty air, passed on through the forest, where no church had ever been gathered or solitary Christian prayed. Whither, then, could these holy men be journeying so deep into the heathen wilderness? Young Goodman Brown caught hold of a tree for support, being ready to sink down on the ground, faint and overburdened with the heavy sickness of his heart. He looked up to the sky, doubting whether there really was a heaven above him. Yet there was the blue arch, and the stars brightening in it.

"With heaven above and Faith below, I will yet stand firm against the devil!" cried Goodman Brown.

While he still gazed upward into the deep arch of the firmament and had lifted his hands to pray, a cloud, though no wind was stirring, hurried across the zenith and hid the brightening stars. The blue sky was still visible, except directly overhead, where this black mass of cloud was sweeping swiftly northward. Aloft in the air, as if from the depths of the cloud, came a confused and doubtful sound of voices. Once the listener fancied that he could distinguish the accents of towns-people of his own, men and women, both pious and ungodly, many of whom he had met at the communion table, and had seen others rioting at the tavern. The next moment, so indistinct were the sounds, he doubted whether he had heard aught but the murmur of the old forest, whispering without a wind. Then came a stronger swell of those familiar tones, heard daily in the sunshine at Salem village, but never until now from a cloud of night. There was one voice, of a young woman, uttering lamentations, yet with an uncertain sorrow, and entreating for some favor, which, perhaps, it would grieve her to obtain; and all the unseen multitude, both saints and sinners, seemed to encourage her onward.

"Faith!" shouted Goodman Brown, in a voice of agony and desperation; and the echoes of the forest mocked him, crying, "Faith! Faith!" as if bewildered wretches were seeking her all through the wilderness.

The cry of grief, rage, and terror was yet piercing the night, when the unhappy husband held his breath for a response. There was a scream, drowned immediately in a louder murmur of voices, fading into far-off laughter, as the dark cloud swept away, leaving the clear and silent sky above Goodman Brown. But something fluttered lightly down through the air and caught on the branch of a tree. The young man seized it, and beheld a pink ribbon.

"My Faith is gone!" cried he after one stupefied moment. "There is no good on earth; and sin is but a name. Come, devil; for to thee is this world given."

And, maddened with despair, so that he laughed loud and long, did Goodman Brown grasp his staff and set forth again, at such a rate that he seemed to fly along the forest path rather than to walk or run. The road grew wilder and drearier and more faintly traced, and vanished at length, leaving him in the heart of the dark wilderness, still rushing onward with the instinct that guides mortal man to evil. The whole forest was peopled with frightful sounds—the creaking of the trees, the howling of wild beasts, and the yell of Indians; while sometimes the wind tolled like a distant church bell, and sometimes gave a broad roar around the traveller, as if all Nature were laughing him to scorn. But he was himself the chief horror of the scene, and shrank not from its other horrors.

"Ha! ha! ha!" roared Goodman Brown when the wind laughed at him. "Let us hear which will laugh loudest. Think not to frighten me with your deviltry. Come witch, come wizard, come Indian powwow, come devil himself, and here comes Goodman Brown. You may as well fear him as he fear you."

In truth, all through the haunted forest there could be nothing more frightful than the figure of Goodman Brown. On he flew among the black pines, brandishing his staff with frenzied gestures, now giving vent to an inspiration of horrid blasphemy, and now shouting forth such laughter as set all the echoes of the forest laughing like demons around him. The fiend in his own shape is less hideous than when he rages in the breast of man. Thus sped the demoniac on his course, until, quivering among the trees, he saw a red light before him, as when the felled trunks and branches of a clearing have been set on fire, and throw up their lurid blaze against the sky, at the hour of midnight. He paused, in a lull of the tempest that had driven him onward, and heard the swell of what seemed a hymn, rolling solemnly from a distance with the weight of many voices. He knew the tune; it was a familiar one in the choir of the village meeting-house. The verse died heavily away, and was lengthened by a chorus, not of human voices, but of all the sounds of the benighted wilderness pealing in awful harmony together. Goodman Brown cried out, and his cry was lost to his own ear by its unison with the cry of the desert.

In the interval of silence he stole forward until the light glared full upon his eyes. At one extremity of an open space, hemmed in by the dark wall of the forest, arose a rock, bearing some rude, natural resemblance either to an altar or a pulpit, and surrounded by four blazing pines, their tops aflame, their stems untouched, like candles at an evening meeting. The mass of foliage that had overgrown the summit of the rock was all on fire, blazing high into the night and fitfully illuminating the whole field. Each pendent twig and leafy festoon was in a blaze. As the red light arose and fell, a numerous congregation alternately shone forth, then disappeared in shadow, and again grew, as it were, out of the darkness, peopling the heart of the solitary woods at once.

"A grave and dark-clad company," quoth Goodman Brown.

In truth they were such. Among them, quivering to and fro between gloom and splendor, appeared faces that would be seen next day at the council board of the province, and others which, Sabbath after Sabbath, looked devoutly heavenward, and benignantly over the crowded pews, from the holiest pulpits in the land. Some affirm that the lady of the governor was there. At least there were high dames well known to her, and wives of honored husbands, and widows, a great multitude, and ancient maidens, all of excellent repute, and fair young girls, who trembled lest their mothers should espy them. Either the sudden gleams of light flashing over the obscure field bedazzled Goodman Brown, or he recognized a score of the church members of Salem village famous for their especial sanctity. Good old Deacon Gookin had arrived, and waited at the skirts of that venerable saint, his revered pastor. But, irreverently consorting with these grave, reputable, and pious people, these elders of the church, these chaste dames and dewy virgins, there were men of dissolute lives and women of spotted fame, wretches given over to all mean and filthy vice, and suspected even of horrid crimes. It was strange to see that the good shrank not from the wicked, nor were the sinners abashed by the saints. Scattered also among their pale-faced enemies were the Indian priests, or powwows, who had often scared their native forest with more hideous incantations than any known to English witchcraft.

"But where is Faith?" thought Goodman Brown; and, as hope came into his heart, he trembled.

Another verse of the hymn arose, a slow and mournful strain, such as the pious love, but joined to words which expressed all that our nature can conceive of sin, and darkly hinted at far more. Unfathomable to mere mortals is the lore of fiends. Verse after verse was sung; and still the chorus of the desert swelled between like the deepest tone of a mighty organ; and with the final peal of that dreadful anthem there came a sound, as if the roaring wind, the rushing streams, the howling beasts, and every other voice of the unconcerted wilderness were mingling and according with the voice of guilty man in homage to the prince of all. The four blazing pines threw up a loftier flame, and obscurely discovered shapes and visages of horror on the smoke wreaths above the impious assembly. At the same moment the fire on the rock shot redly forth and formed a flowing arch above its base, where now appeared a figure. With reverence be it spoken, the figure bore no slight similitude, both in garb and manner, to some grave divine of the New England churches.

"Bring forth the converts!" cried a voice that echoed through the field and rolled into the forest.

At the word, Goodman Brown stepped forth from the shadow of the trees and approached the congregation, with whom he felt a loathful brotherhood by the sympathy of all that was wicked in his heart. He could have well-nigh sworn that the shape of his own dead father beckoned him to advance, looking downward from a smoke wreath, while a woman, with dim features of despair, threw out her hand to warn him back. Was it his mother? But he had no power to retreat one step, nor to resist, even in thought, when the minister and good old Deacon Gookin seized his arms and led him to the blazing rock. Thither came also the slender form of a veiled female, led between Goody Cloyse, that pious teacher of the catechism, and Martha Carrier, who had received the devil's promise to be queen of hell. A rampant hag was she. And there stood the proselytes beneath the canopy of fire.

"Welcome, my children," said the dark figure, "to the communion of your race. Ye have found thus young your nature and your destiny. My children, look behind you!"

They turned; and flashing forth, as it were, in a sheet of flame, the fiend worshippers were seen; the smile of welcome gleamed darkly on every visage.

"There," resumed the sable form, "are all whom ye have reverenced from youth. Ye deemed them holier than yourselves and shrank from your own sin, contrasting it with their lives of righteousness and prayerful aspirations heavenward. Yet here are they all in my worshipping assembly. This night it shall be granted you to know their secret deeds: how hoary-bearded elders of the church have whispered wanton words to the young maids of their households; how many a woman, eager for widows' weeds, has given her husband a drink at bedtime and let him sleep his last sleep in her bosom; how beardless youths have made haste to inherit their fathers' wealth; and how fair damsels—blush not, sweet ones—have dug little graves in the garden, and bidden me, the sole guest, to an infant's funeral. By the sympathy of your human hearts for sin ye shall scent out all the places—whether in church, bedchamber, street, field, or forest—where crime has been committed, and shall exult to behold the whole earth one stain of guilt, one mighty blood spot. Far more than this. It shall be yours to penetrate, in every bosom, the deep mystery of sin, the fountain of all wicked arts, and which inexhaustibly supplies more evil impulses than human power—than my power at its utmost—can make manifest in deeds. And now, my children, look upon each other."

They did so; and, by the blaze of the hell-kindled torches, the wretched man beheld his Faith, and the wife her husband, trembling before that unhallowed altar.

"Lo, there ye stand, my children," said the figure, in a deep and solemn tone, almost sad with its despairing awfulness, as if his once angelic nature could yet mourn for our miserable race. "Depending upon one another's hearts, ye had still hoped that virtue were not all a dream. Now are ye undeceived. Evil is the nature of mankind. Evil must be your only happiness. Welcome again, my children, to the communion of your race."

"Welcome," repeated the fiend worshippers, in one cry of despair and triumph.

And there they stood, the only pair, as it seemed, who were yet hesitating on the verge of wickedness in this dark world. A basin was hallowed, naturally, in the rock. Did it contain water, reddened by the lurid light? or was it blood? or, perchance, a liquid flame? Herein did the shape of evil dip his hand and prepare to lay the mark of baptism upon their foreheads, that they might be partakers of the mystery of sin, more conscious of the secret guilt of others, both in deed and thought, than they could now be of their own. The husband cast one look at his pale wife, and Faith at him. What polluted wretches would the next glance show them to each other, shuddering alike at what they disclosed and what they saw!

"Faith! Faith!" cried the husband, "look up to heaven, and resist the wicked one."

Whether Faith obeyed he knew not. Hardly had he spoken when he found himself amid calm night and solitude, listening to a roar of the wind which died heavily away through the forest. He staggered against the rock, and felt it chill and damp; while a hanging twig, that had been all on fire, besprinkled his cheek with the coldest dew.

The next morning young Goodman Brown came slowly into the street of Salem village, staring around him like a bewildered man. The good old minister was taking a walk along the graveyard to get an appetite for breakfast and meditate his sermon, and bestowed a blessing, as he passed, on Goodman Brown. He shrank from the venerable saint as if to avoid an anathema. Old Deacon Gookin was at domestic worship, and the holy words of his prayer were heard through the open window. "What God doth the wizard pray to?" quoth Goodman Brown. Goody Cloyse, that excellent old Christian, stood in the early sunshine at her own lattice, catechizing a little girl who had brought her a pint of morning's milk. Goodman Brown snatched away the child as from the grasp of the fiend himself. Turning the corner by the meeting-house, he spied the head of Faith, with the pink ribbons, gazing anxiously forth, and bursting into such joy at sight of him that she skipped along the street and almost kissed her husband before the whole village. But Goodman Brown looked sternly and sadly into her face, and passed on without a greeting.

Had Goodman Brown fallen asleep in the forest and only dreamed a wild dream of a witch-meeting?

Be it so if you will; but, alas! it was a dream of evil omen for young Goodman Brown. A stern, a sad, a darkly meditative, a distrustful, if not a desperate man did he become from the night of that fearful dream. On the Sabbath day, when the congregation were singing a holy psalm, he could not listen because an anthem of sin rushed loudly upon his ear and drowned all the blessed strain. When the minister spoke from the pulpit with power and fervid eloquence, and, with his hand on the open Bible, of the sacred truths of our religion, and of saint-like lives and triumphant deaths, and of future bliss or misery unutterable, then did Goodman Brown turn pale, dreading lest the roof should thunder down upon the gray blasphemer and his hearers. Often, awaking suddenly at midnight, he shrank from the bosom of Faith; and at morning or eventide, when the family knelt down at prayer, he scowled and muttered to himself, and gazed sternly at his wife, and turned away. And when he had lived long, and was borne to his grave a hoary corpse, followed by Faith, an aged woman, and children and grandchildren, a goodly procession, besides neighbors not a few, they carved no hopeful verse upon his tombstone, for his dying hour was gloom.

[1835]

Lit. for Reason

MICHAEL LEVIN   [b. 1943]

The Case for Torture

Libertarian writer and educator **Michael Levin** was born in Brooklyn, New York, and earned his Ph.D. from Columbia University. Currently he is a professor of philosophy at the City College of New York. His controversial work includes *Feminism and Freedom* (1987), a condemnation of affirmative action, and *Why Race Matters: Race Differences and What They Mean* (1997), in which he argues for racial differences in ability and personality.

Levin's provocative essay "The Case for Torture," first published in *Newsweek* in 1982, makes a case for the eleventh-hour torture of terrorists if the result is the preservation of innocent lives. Levin does not deny that torturing a terrorist is unconstitutional, but when weighed against the immediate possibility of mass murder, he thinks, constitutionality is not the foremost concern. Condemning "moral cowards" who deem the terrorist's life sacred at the cost of any number of innocent lives, Levin writes, "If life is so valuable that it must never be taken, the lives of the innocents must be saved even at the price of hurting the one who endangers them."

It is generally assumed that torture is impermissible, a throwback to a more brutal age. Enlightened societies reject it outright, and regimes suspected of using it risk the wrath of the United States.

I believe this attitude is unwise.|There are situations in which torture is not merely permissible but morally mandatory.|Moreover, these situations are moving from the realm of imagination to fact.

Suppose a terrorist has hidden an atomic bomb on Manhattan Island which will detonate at noon on July 4 unless...(here follow the usual demands for money and release of his friends from jail). Suppose, further, that he is caught at 10 a.m. of the fateful day, but—preferring death to failure—won't disclose where the bomb is. What do we do? If we follow due process—wait for his lawyer, arraign him—millions of people will die. If the only way to save those lives is to subject the terrorist to the most excruciating possible pain, what grounds can there be for not

Michael Levin, "The Case for Torture" from *Newsweek*, June 7, 1982. Reprinted by permission of the author.

doing so? I suggest there are none. In any case, I ask you to face the question with an open mind.

Torturing the terrorist is unconstitutional? Probably. But millions of lives surely outweigh constitutionality. Torture is barbaric? Mass murder is far more barbaric. Indeed, letting millions of innocents die in deference to one who flaunts his guilt is moral cowardice, an unwillingness to dirty one's hands. If *you* caught the terrorist, could you sleep nights knowing that millions died because you couldn't bring yourself to apply the electrodes?

Once you concede that torture is justified in extreme cases, you have 5 admitted that the decision to use torture is a matter of balancing innocent lives against the means needed to save them. You must now face more realistic cases involving more modest numbers. Someone plants a bomb on a jumbo jet. He alone can disarm it, and his demands cannot be met (or if they can, we refuse to set a precedent by yielding to his threats). Surely we can, we must, do anything to the extortionist to save the passengers. How can we tell three hundred, or one hundred, or ten people who never asked to be put in danger, "I'm sorry, you'll have to die in agony, we just couldn't bring ourselves to..."

Here are the results of an informal poll about a third, hypothetical, case. Suppose a terrorist group kidnapped a newborn baby from a hospital. I asked four mothers if they would approve of torturing the kidnappers if that were necessary to get their own newborns back. All said yes, the most "liberal" adding that she would like to administer it herself.

I am not advocating torture as punishment. Punishment is addressed to deeds irrevocably past. Rather, I am advocating torture as an acceptable measure for preventing future evils. So understood, it is far less objectionable than many extant punishments. Opponents of the death penalty, for example, are forever insisting that executing a murderer will not bring back his victim (as if the purpose of capital punishment were supposed to be resurrection, not deterrence or retribution). But torture, in the cases described, is intended not to bring anyone back but to keep innocents from being dispatched. The most powerful argument against using torture as a punishment or to secure confessions is that such practices disregard the rights of the individual. Well, if the individual is all that important—and he is—it is correspondingly important to protect the rights of individuals threatened by terrorists. If life is so valuable that it must never be taken, the lives of the innocents must be saved even at the price of hurting the one who endangers them.

Better precedents for torture are assassination and preemptive attack. No Allied leader would have flinched at assassinating Hitler, had that been possible. (The Allies did assassinate Heydrich.) Americans would be angered to learn that Roosevelt could have had Hitler killed in 1943—

thereby shortening the war and saving millions of lives—but refused on moral grounds. Similarly, if nation A learns that nation B is about to launch an unprovoked attack, A has a right to save itself by destroying B's military capability first. In the same way, if the police can by torture save those who would otherwise die at the hands of kidnappers or terrorists, they must.

There is an important difference between terrorists and their victims that should mute talk of the terrorists' "rights." The terrorist's victims are at risk unintentionally, not having asked to be endangered. But the terrorist knowingly initiated his actions. Unlike his victims, he volunteered for the risks of his deed. By threatening to kill for profit or idealism, he renounces civilized standards, and he can have no complaint if civilization tries to thwart him by whatever means necessary.

Just as torture is justified only to save lives (not extort confessions or 10 recantations), it is justifiably administered only to those *known* to hold innocent lives in their hands. Ah, but how can the authorities ever be sure they have the right malefactor? Isn't there a danger of error and abuse? Won't We turn into Them?

Questions like these are disingenuous in a world in which terrorists proclaim themselves and perform for television. The name of their game is public recognition. After all, you can't very well intimidate a government into releasing your freedom fighters unless you announce that it is your group that has seized its embassy. "Clear guilt" is difficult to define, but when forty million people see a group of masked gunmen seize an airplane on the evening news, there is not much question about who the perpetrators are. There will be hard cases where the situation is murkier. Nonetheless, a line demarcating the legitimate use of torture can be drawn. Torture only the obviously guilty, and only for the sake of saving innocents, and the line between Us and Them will remain clear.

There is little danger that the Western democracies will lose their way if they choose to inflict pain as one way of preserving order. Paralysis in the face of evil is the greater danger. Some day soon a terrorist will threaten tens of thousands of lives, and torture will be the only way to save them. We had better start thinking about this.

124

CLINTON R. VAN ZANDT

It Should Be Permissible to Torture Suspected Terrorists to Gather Information

Clinton R. Van Zandt is a twenty-five year veteran of the FBI, where he was the chief hostage negotiator and manager of the Major Case/ Crisis Management Program. As a supervisor of the Behavioral Science or "Silence of the Lambs" Unit, Van Zandt was the lead hostage negotiator in many national and international hostage situations, including the 1993 siege at the Branch Davidian Compound in Waco, Texas. He was also instrumental in the identification and capture of the "Unabomber" and the correct profiling of Oklahoma City bomber Timothy McVeigh. A former agent with U.S. Army Intelligence and a Vietnam veteran, Clinton earned his B.S. from Southern Illinois University and his M.A. and Ph.D. from The State University of New York. His book *Dynamic Processes of Crisis Negotiation* was awarded the 1998 Best Book Award by The International Association for Conflict Management. A popular television and radio commentator and lecturer in crisis management, terrorist situations, hostage negotiations, and other security related matters, Van Zandt is the president of Van Zandt Associates, Inc., a risk and threat assessment group specializing in behavioral and forensic analyses.

First published in *CQ Researcher* in 2003, "It Should Be Permissible to Torture Suspected Terrorists to Gather Information" is Van Zandt's proposal that a national court be developed by the government to authorize the use of torture in certain cases of national security in order to maintain public safety. With the court's issuance of a "duress-interview warrant," exempt from appeal or public scrutiny, the safeguarding of national security would take priority over the preservation of a suspect's human rights.

Clinton R. Van Zandt, "It Should Be Permissible to Torture Suspected Terrorists to Gather Information." From *Torture*, the April 18, 2003 report of *CQ Researcher*. Visit www.cqresearcher.com for the complete report. Used by permission of CQ Press, a division of Congressional Quarterly, Inc.

In man's search for truth down through the ages, "trial by ordeal" often has been resorted to when a suspect refused to talk. In recent times, however, numerous nations and international bodies have legislated against the intentional infliction of pain or suffering in an attempt to gain information or a confession.

Most civilized people would say they oppose the inhuman or degrading treatment of another human being. But what happens when there is a so-called "ticking time bomb"—a situation when a suspect is thought to have time-sensitive information affecting the lives of thousands—or even millions—of people? When the ticking bomb is factored into the equation, the physical and psychological rules of engagement suddenly become a sticky sea of gray for many otherwise absolutists.

The U.S. once taught friendly governments how to extract information from prisoners by the use of coercive techniques known as "stress and duress." Interview strategies were designed to exhaust the individual's ability to resist while providing him with the rationalization he needed to cooperate.

In the war against terrorism, we seek to gain intelligence about our adversary of immediate as well as long-term strategic value. In both cloak-and-dagger missions and law-enforcement operations, there may come a time when our nation must quickly try to obtain information critical to the lives of millions of people from a person who refuses to talk.

To remain a nation based upon the rule of law, the United States needs 5 to establish a court at the national level before which the government could argue that torture was essential to extract critical information. The court would be required to rule on the matter immediately, and if in agreement, it would be able to issue a "duress-interview warrant" allowing the authorities to do whatever was necessary to obtain the needed information from the prisoner. There would be no appeal process and no public or media scrutiny. The authority of the court would be absolute.

In short, the overriding public-safety issue would take precedence over a prisoner's human rights. Without such a mechanism, we are left with conventional methods of interrogation while watching the seconds on the time bomb tick away, as the only person who might know how to stop the clock remains mute and simply awaits our fate. And lastly, should time allow, we still need to verify and corroborate the information before we act on it.

PHILIP B. HEYMANN

Torture Should
Not Be Authorized

A former Fulbright Scholar, **Philip B. Heymann** received his B.A. in
philosophy from Yale University and his J.D. from Harvard Law School
in 1960. Having spent much of his career in government, Heymann has,
among other duties, served as the associate prosecutor and consultant
to the Watergate Special Task Force and the U.S. deputy attorney general during the Clinton administration. He has written extensively on
public policy, specializing in criminal law, law enforcement, and terrorism. His books include *The Politics of Public Management* (1987), *Terrorism, Freedom, and Security* (2003), and, with coauthor Juliette Kayyem,
Protecting Liberty in an Age of Terror (2005). He is currently the James
Barr Ames Professor of Law at Harvard University.

In his essay "Torture Should Not Be Authorized," Heymann argues
that it is better to keep the international ban on torture intact than to
make allowances, even with the approval of judges. The potential harm,
he writes, far outweighs the possibility of sometimes obtaining useful
information.

Authorizing torture is a bad and dangerous idea that can easily be made
to sound plausible. There is a subtle fallacy embedded in the traditional
"ticking bomb" argument for torture to save lives.

That argument goes like this. First, I can imagine dangers so dire that
I might torture or kill guilty or innocent persons if I was quite sure that
was necessary and sufficient to prevent those dangers. Second, very
many feel this way, although differing in the circumstances and the certainty level they would want. Therefore, the "ticking bomb" argument
concludes, everyone wants a system for authorizing torture or murder;
we need only debate the circumstances and the level of certainty.

This conclusion, leading to abandonment of one of the few worldwide
legal prohibitions, leaves out the fact that I do not have faith in the
authorizing system for finding the required circumstances with any
certainty because the costs of errors are born by the suspect tortured,

Philip B. Heymann. "Torture Should Not Be Authorized" from *The Boston Globe*,
February 16, 2002. Reprinted by permission of the author.

127

not by those who decide to torture him. The conclusion also ignores the high probability that the practice of torture will spread unwisely if acceptance of torture with the approval of judges is substituted for a flat, worldwide prohibition.

The use of torture would increase sharply if there were "torture warrants." Any law enforcement or intelligence official who tortures a prisoner in the United States now is very likely to be prosecuted and imprisoned.

Punches may be thrown, but anything we think of as "torture" is con- 5 sidered an inexcusable practice. That revulsion will disappear if we make torture acceptable and legal whenever a judge accepts the judgment of intelligence officials that: (1) there is a bomb; (2) the suspect knows where it is; (3) torture will get the truth, not a false story, out of him before the bomb explodes; (4) the bomb won't be moved in the meantime. Every individual who believes in his heart, however recklessly, that those conditions (or others he thinks are just as compelling) are met will think there is nothing seriously wrong with torture.

Professor Alan Dershowitz wants to bet that judges will say "no" in a high enough percentage of cases of "ticking bombs" that whatever moral force their refusal has will offset the legitimating and demoralizing effects of authorizing occasional torture. It's a bad bet.

Judges have deferred to the last several thousand requests for national security wiretaps and they would defer here. The basis of their decisions, information revealing secret "sources and methods" of intelligence gathering, would not be public. And if the judge refused, overrode the judgment of agents who thought lives would be lost without torture, and denied a warrant, why would that decision be more likely to be accepted and followed by agents desperate to save lives than the flat ban on torture we now have?

How many false positives do you want to accept? You would get six false positives out of 10 occasions of torture even in the extraordinarily unlikely event that the intelligence officers convince the judge that they were really 80 percent sure of each of the above four predictions.

And even if you would tolerate this number of false positives if torture were in fact the only way to get the needed information to defuse the bomb, there are frequently other promising ways (such as emergency searches or stimulating conversations over tapped phones) that will be abandoned or discounted if torture is available.

Finally, if we approve torture in one set of circumstances, isn't every 10 country then free to define its own exceptions, applicable to Americans as well as its own citizens? Fear of that led us to accept the Geneva Convention prohibiting torture of a prisoner of war, although obtaining his information might save dozens of American lives.

As to preventing terrorism, torture is an equally bad idea. Torture is a prescription for losing a war for support of our beliefs in the hope of reducing the casualties from relatively small battles. Dershowitz misunderstands my argument. I do not accept torture either "off the books" with a wink at the secret discretion of the torturers or on the open authority of the judges from whom they might seek authorization. I predict so many types of harms to so many people and to the nation from any system that authorizes torture, either secretly or openly, that I would prohibit it. The overall, longer-term cost of any system authorizing torture, openly or tacitly, would far outweigh its occasional, short-term benefits.

VINCENT IACOPINO

It Should Not Be
Permitted to Torture
Suspected Terrorists to
Gather Information

Vincent Iacopino, M.D., Ph.D., is an expert in the field of health and human rights. A former Robert Wood Johnson Clinical Scholar at Stanford University, Iacopino specializes in internal medicine and has conducted investigations into human rights violations in eleven different locations, including Turkey, South Africa, Kosovo, and Chechnya. He is particularly interested in the relationship between health and human rights and has written extensively on the subject. He also served as the Medical Director of Survivors International, a nonprofit organization that provides assistance to survivors of torture. Iacopino currently teaches at the University of California, Berkeley School of Public Health and serves as the Director of Research for Physicians for Human Rights, or PHR.

In the following essay, Iacopino asserts that torture can never be justified. If the United States is either silent on the subject or complicit in the practice of torture, he contends, we are likely to lose our humanity.

Torture cannot be justified by any government, for any reason, despite recent reports of U.S. officials and others attempting to justify such practices. Torture is unequivocally prohibited in international law. This legal and moral imperative was established in the aftermath of Nazi war crimes as a rhetorical statement of moral and human identity. Under the U.N. Convention against Torture, the United States is obligated to prohibit torture, ensure prompt and impartial investigations and prosecute perpetrators. Additionally, on countless occasions the State Department's Country Report on Human Rights Practices has criticized governments that torture, in some cases the same practices the U.S. is now accused of committing in its "war on terrorism."

Vincent Iacopino, "It Should Not Be Permitted to Torture Suspected Terrorists to Gather Information." From *Torture*, the April 18, 2003 report of *CQ Researcher*. Visit www.cqresearcher.com for the complete report. Used by permission of CQ Press, a division of Congressional Quarterly, Inc.

Those now advocating the use of torture risk undermining principles of justice and the rule of law in what appears to be an unfortunate public display of arrogance and ignorance:

- Torture does not make any one person or society safer or more secure. States that torture undermine their authority and legitimacy. Also, U.S. sanctioning of any form of torture will escalate its already widespread use.

- Those currently arguing in the abstract for torture only under "special circumstances" or with "humane limitations" know very little of the horror they are prescribing. Even seemingly innocuous methods of torture such as hooding can be terrorizing—for example, when combined with a mock execution or other psychological methods. Moreover, hypothetical "limits" on torture cannot be ensured in the absence of independent monitoring of all interactions with detainees and investigation and prosecution of all allegations of torture—conditions that torturers do not permit.

- Labeling torture as a "stress and duress" interrogation technique does not alter the brutality that it represents.

- "Ticking bomb" scenarios are naive, abstract fantasies that serve to assuage the moral conscience of perpetrators and collaborators.

Acts of terror must be prevented and punished. To consider using acts of torture that the world has deemed unacceptable under any circumstance is profoundly disturbing. Torture will never serve the interests of justice because it undermines the dignity of us all. We all lose when the "war on terrorism" ends up threatening the protection of human rights.

The United States must be neither silent nor, in any way, complicit with such practices, or, indeed, we risk losing that which we seek to preserve— our humanity.

EDGAR ALLAN POE   [1809–1849]

The Tell-Tale Heart

Born in Boston, Massachusetts, **Edgar Allan Poe** was the son of itinerant actors, abandoned at one year of age by his father; his mother died soon after. He became the ward of John Allan of Richmond, Virginia, whose surname became Poe's middle name. When the family fortunes declined, the Allans moved to England. Poe was educated there and at the new University of Virginia upon his return to Richmond. Although an excellent student, Poe drank and gambled heavily, causing his withdrawal from the university after one year. Poe made his way to Boston, enlisted in the army, and took an appointment at West Point. After further dissipation ended his military career, Poe set out to support himself by writing. Three volumes of poetry brought in little money, and in 1835 Poe took a position as an assistant editor of the *Southern Literary Messenger*, the first of many positions lost because of drinking. He then began to publish short stories, and in 1836 he married his thirteen-year-old cousin, Virginia Clemm, and took on the support of her mother, increasing his financial difficulties. They went to New York City, where Poe published *The Narrative of Arthur Gordon Pym* (1838) and *Tales of the Grotesque and Arabesque* (1840), his first story collection. At that time he began to write detective stories, virtually inventing a genre. Already respected as a critic, Poe won fame as a poet with *The Raven and Other Poems* (1845). In 1847, after his wife died, Poe became engaged to the poet Sarah Helen Whitman, who ultimately resisted the marriage because of his drinking problem. In 1849 Poe met a childhood sweetheart, Elmira Royster Shelton, who agreed to marry him. After celebrating his apparent reversal of fortune with friends in Baltimore, he was found unconscious in the street and died shortly thereafter. Always admired in Europe, Poe's major stories of horror and detection, poems, and critical pieces on the craft of writing are considered American classics. "The Tell-Tale Heart" was first published in James Russell Lowell's *Pioneer*, a Boston literary magazine, in February 1843. It is, perhaps, the most famous of Poe's short stories and has been adapted many times for film and television.

True!—nervous—very, very dreadfully nervous I had been and am; but why *will* you say that I am mad? The disease had sharpened my senses—not destroyed—not dulled them. Above all was the sense of hearing acute. I heard all things in the heaven and in the earth. I heard many things in hell. How, then, am I mad? Hearken! and observe how healthily—how calmly I can tell you the whole story.

It is impossible to say how first the idea entered my brain; but once conceived, it haunted me day and night. Object there was none. Passion there was none. I loved the old man. He had never wronged me. He had never given me insult. For his gold I had no desire. I think it was his eye! yes, it was this! One of his eyes resembled that of a vulture—a pale blue eye, with a film over it. Whenever it fell upon me, my blood ran cold; and so by degrees—very gradually—I made up my mind to take the life of the old man, and thus rid myself of the eye for ever.

Now this is the point. You fancy me mad. Madmen know nothing. But you should have seen *me*. You should have seen how wisely I proceeded—with what caution—with what foresight—with what dissimulation I went to work! I was never kinder to the old man than during the whole week before I killed him. And every right, about midnight, I turned the latch of his door and opened it—oh, so gently! And then, when I had made an opening sufficient for my head, I put in a dark lantern, all closed, so that no light shone out, and then I thrust in my head. Oh, you would have laughed to see how cunningly I thrust it in! I moved it slowly—very, very slowly, so that I might not disturb the old man's sleep. It took me an hour to place my whole head within the opening so far that I could see him as he lay upon his bed. Ha—would a madman have been so wise as this? And then; when my head was well in the room, I undid the lantern cautiously—oh, so cautiously—cautiously (for the hinges creaked)—I undid it just so much that a single thin ray fell upon the vulture eye. And this I did for seven long nights—every night just after midnight—but I found the eye always closed; and so it was impossible to do the work; for it was not the old man who vexed me, but his Evil Eye. And every morning, when the day broke, I went boldly into the chamber, and spoke courageously to him, calling him by name in a hearty tone, and inquiring how he had passed the night. So you see he would have been a very profound old man, indeed, to suspect that every night, just at twelve, I looked in upon him while he slept.

Upon the eighth night I was more than usually cautious in opening the door. A watch's minute hand moves more quickly than did mine. Never before that night had I *felt* the extent of my own powers—of my sagacity. I could scarcely contain my feelings of triumph. To think that there I was, opening the door, little by little, and he not even to dream of my secret deeds or thoughts. I fairly chuckled at the idea; and perhaps he heard me; for he moved on the bed suddenly, as if startled. Now you may think that I drew back—but no. His room was as black as pitch with the thick darkness (for the shutters were close fastened, through fear of robbers), and so I knew that he could not see the opening of the door, and I kept pushing it on steadily, steadily.

I had my head in, and was about to open the lantern, when my thumb 5 slipped upon the tin fastening, and the old man sprang up in the bed, crying out—"Who's there?"

I kept quite still and said nothing. For a whole hour I did not move a muscle, and in the meantime I did not hear him lie down. He was still sitting up in the bed listening;—just as I have done, night after night, hearkening to the death watches in the wall.

Presently I heard a slight groan, and I knew it was the groan of mortal terror. It was not a groan of pain or of grief—oh, no!—it was the low stifled sound that arises from the bottom of the soul when overcharged with awe. I knew the sound well. Many a night, just at midnight, when all the world slept, it has welled up from my own bosom, deepening with its dreadful echo, the terrors that distracted me. I say I knew it well. I knew what the old man felt, and pitied him, although I chuckled at heart. I knew that he had been lying awake ever since the first slight noise, when he had turned in the bed. His fears had been ever since growing upon him. He had been trying to fancy them causeless, but could not. He had been saying to himself—"It is nothing but the wind in the chimney—it is only a mouse crossing the floor," or "it is merely a cricket which has made a single chirp." Yes, he has been trying to comfort himself with these suppositions; but he had found all in vain. *All in vain*; because Death, in approaching him, had stalked with his black shadow before him, and enveloped the victim. And it was the mournful influence of the unperceived shadow that caused him to feel—although he neither saw nor heard—to *feel* the presence of my head within the room.

When I had waited a long time, very patiently, without hearing him lie down, I resolved to open a little—a very, very little crevice in the lantern. So I opened it—you cannot imagine how stealthily, stealthily—until, at length, a single dim ray, like the thread of the spider, shot from out the crevice and full upon the vulture eye.

It was open—wide, wide open—and I grew furious as I gazed upon it. I saw it with perfect distinctness—all a dull blue, with a hideous veil over it that chilled the very marrow in my bones, but I could see nothing else of the old man's face or person: for I had directed the ray as if by instinct, precisely upon the damned spot.

And now have I not told you that what you mistake for madness is but 10 over-acuteness of the senses?—now, I say, there came to my ears a low, dull, quick sound, such as a watch makes when enveloped in cotton. I knew *that* sound well too. It was the beating of the old man's heart. It

134

increased my fury, as the beating of a drum stimulates the soldier into courage.

But even yet I refrained and kept still. I scarcely breathed. I held the lantern motionless. I tried how steadily I could maintain the ray upon the eye. Meantime the hellish tattoo of the heart increased. It grew quicker and quicker, and louder and louder every instant. The old man's terror *must* have been extreme! It grew louder, I say, louder every moment!—do you mark me well? I have told you that I am nervous: so I am. And now at the dead hour of the night, amid the dreadful silence of that old house, so strange a noise as this excited me to uncontrollable terror. Yet, for some minutes longer I refrained and stood still. But the beating grew louder louder! I thought the heart must burst. And now a new anxiety seized me—the sound would be heard by a neighbor! The old man's hour had come! With a loud yell, I threw open the lantern and leaped into the room. He shrieked once—once only. In an instant I dragged him to the floor, and pulled the heavy bed over him. I then smiled gaily, to find the deed so far done. But, for many minutes, the heart beat on with a muffled sound. This, however, did not vex me; it would not be heard through the wall. At length it ceased. The old man was dead. I removed the bed and examined the corpse. Yes, he was stone, stone dead. I placed my hand upon the heart and held it there many minutes. There was no pulsation. He was stone dead. His eye would trouble me no more.

If still you think me mad, you will think so no longer when I describe the wise precautions I took for the concealment of the body. The night waned, and I worked hastily, but in silence. First of all I dismembered the corpse. I cut off the head and the arms and the legs.

I then took up three planks from the flooring of the chamber, and deposited all between the scantlings. I then replaced the boards so cleverly, so cunningly, that no human eye—not even *his*—could have detected anything wrong. There was nothing to wash out—no stain of any kind—no blood-spot whatever. I had been too wary for that. A tub had caught all—ha! ha!

When I had made an end of these labors, it was four o'clock—still dark as midnight. As the bell sounded the hour, there came a knocking at the street door. I went down to open it with a light heart—for what had I *now* to fear? There entered three men, who introduced themselves, with perfect suavity, as officers of the police. A shriek had been heard by a neighbor during the night; suspicion of foul play had been aroused; information had been lodged at the police office, and they (the officers) had been deputed to search the premises.

I smiled—for *what* had I to fear? I bade the gentlemen welcome. The shriek, I said, was my own in a dream. The old man, I mentioned, was 15

135

absent in the country. I took my visitors all over the house. I bade them search—search *well*. I led them, at length, to *his* chamber. I showed them his treasures, secure, undisturbed. In the enthusiasm of my confidence, I brought chairs into the room, and desired them *here* to rest from their fatigues, while I myself, in the wild audacity of my perfect triumph, placed my own seat upon the very spot beneath which reposed the corpse of the victim.

The officers were satisfied. My *manner* had convinced them. I was singularly at ease. They sat, and while I answered cheerily, they chatted familiar things. But, ere long, I felt myself getting pale and wished them gone. My head ached, and I fancied a ringing in my ears: but still they sat and still chatted. The ringing became more distinct:—it continued and became more distinct: I talked more freely to get rid of the feeling: but it continued and gained definitiveness—until, at length, I found that the noise was *not* within my ears.

No doubt I now grew *very* pale;—but I talked more fluently, and with a heightened voice. Yet the sound increased—and what could I do? It was *a low, dull, quick sound—much such a sound as a watch makes when enveloped in cotton.* I gasped for breath—and yet the officers heard it not. I talked more quickly—more vehemently; but the noise steadily increased. I arose and argued about trifles, in a high key and with violent gesticulations, but the noise steadily increased. Why *would* they not be gone? I paced the floor to and fro with heavy strides, as if excited to fury by the observation of the men—but the noise steadily increased. Oh God! what *could* I do? I foamed—I raved—I swore! I swung the chair upon which I had been sitting, and grated it upon the boards, but the noise arose over all and continually increased. It grew louder—louder—*louder!* And still the men chatted pleasantly, and smiled. Was it possible they heard not? Almighty God!—no, no! They heard!—they suspected!—they *knew!*—they were making a mockery of my horror!—this I thought, and this I think. But any thing was better than this agony! Any thing was more tolerable than this derision! I could bear those hypocritical smiles no longer! I felt that I must scream or die!—and now—again!—hark! louder! louder! louder! *louder!*—

"Villains!" I shrieked, "dissemble no more! I admit the deed!—tear up the planks!—here, here!—it is the beating of his hideous heart!"

[1843]

EDGAR ALLAN POE [1809–1849]

The Cask of Amontillado

Born in Boston, Massachusetts, **Edgar Allan Poe** (1809–1849), the son of itinerant actors, was abandoned at one year of age by his father; his mother died soon after. The baby became the ward of John Allan of Richmond, Virginia, whose surname became Poe's middle name. When the family fortunes declined, the Allans moved to England. Poe was educated there and at the new University of Virginia upon his return to Richmond. Although an excellent student, Poe drank and gambled heavily, causing Allan to withdraw him from the university after one year. Poe made his way to Boston, enlisted in the army, and eventually, with Allan's help, took an appointment at West Point. After further dissipation ended his military career, Poe set out to support himself by writing. Three volumes of poetry brought in little money, and in 1835 Poe took a position as an assistant editor of the *Southern Literary Messenger,* the first of many positions he lost because of drinking. He began to publish short stories. In 1836 he married his thirteen-year-old cousin, Virginia Clemm, and took on the support of her mother as well, increasing his financial difficulties. They went to New York City, where Poe published *The Narrative of Arthur Gordon Pym* (1838) and assembled the best stories he had published in magazines in *Tales of the Grotesque and Arabesque* (1840), his first story collection. At that time he also began to write detective stories, virtually inventing the genre. Already respected as a critic, Poe won fame as a poet with *The Raven and Other Poems* (1845). In 1847, after the death of his wife, Poe became engaged to the poet Sarah Helen Whitman, a wealthy widow six years his senior, who ultimately resisted marriage because of Poe's drinking problem. In 1849 Poe met a childhood sweetheart, Elmira Royster Shelton, now a widow, who agreed to marry him. After celebrating his apparent reversal of fortune with friends in Baltimore, he was found unconscious in the street and died shortly thereafter. Always admired in Europe, Poe's major stories of horror and detection, his major poems, and his major critical pieces on the craft of writing are considered American classics.

The thousand injuries of Fortunato I had borne as I best could; but when he ventured upon insult, I vowed revenge. You, who so well know the nature of my soul, will not suppose, however, that I gave utterance to a threat. *At length* I would be avenged; this was a point definitely settled—

but the very definitiveness with which it was resolved precluded the idea of risk. I must not only punish, but punish with impunity. A wrong is unredressed when retribution overtakes its redresser. It is equally unredressed when the avenger fails to make himself felt as such to him who has done the wrong.

It must be understood, that neither by word nor deed had I given Fortunato cause to doubt my good-will. I continued, as was my wont, to smile in his face, and he did not perceive that my smile *now* was at the thought of his immolation.

He had a weak point—this Fortunato—although in other regards he was a man to be respected and even feared. He prided himself on his connoisseurship in wine. Few Italians have the true virtuoso spirit. For the most part their enthusiasm is adopted to suit the time and opportunity—to practise imposture upon the British and Austrian *millionnaires*. In painting and gemmary Fortunato, like his countrymen, was a quack—but in the matter of old wines he was sincere. In this respect I did not differ from him materially: I was skilful in the Italian vintages myself, and bought largely whenever I could.

It was about dusk, one evening during the supreme madness of the carnival season, that I encountered my friend. He accosted me with excessive warmth, for he had been drinking much. The man wore motley. He had on a tight-fitting parti-striped dress, and his head was surmounted by the conical cap and bells. I was so pleased to see him, that I thought I should never have done wringing his hand.

I said to him: "My dear Fortunato, you are luckily met. How remarkably well you are looking to-day! But I have received a pipe° of what passes for Amontillado, and I have my doubts."

"How?" said he. "Amontillado? A pipe? Impossible! And in the middle of the carnival!"

"I have my doubts," I replied; "and I was silly enough to pay the full Amontillado price without consulting you in the matter. You were not to be found, and I was fearful of losing a bargain."

"Amontillado!"

"I have my doubts."

"Amontillado!"

"And I must satisfy them."

"Amontillado!"

"As you are engaged, I am on my way to Luchesi. If any one has a critical turn, it is he. He will tell me——"

"Luchesi cannot tell Amontillado from Sherry."

Pipe: A large cask.

"And yet some fools will have it that his taste is a match for your own."

"Come, let us go."

"Whither?"

"To your vaults."

"My friend, no; I will not impose upon your good nature. I perceive you have an engagement. Luchesi——"

"I have no engagement;—come."

"My friend, no. It is not the engagement, but the severe cold with which I perceive you are afflicted. The vaults are insufferably damp. They are encrusted with nitre."

"Let us go, nevertheless. The cold is merely nothing. Amontillado! You have been imposed upon. And as for Luchesi, he cannot distinguish Sherry from Amontillado."

Thus speaking, Fortunato possessed himself of my arm. Putting on a mask of black silk, and drawing a *roquelaire*° closely about my person, I suffered him to hurry me to my palazzo.

There were no attendants at home; they had absconded to make merry in honor of the time. I had told them that I should not return until the morning, and had given them explicit orders not to stir from the house. These orders were sufficient, I well knew, to insure their immediate disappearance, one and all, as soon as my back was turned.

I took from their sconces two flambeaux, and giving one to Fortunato, bowed him through several suites of rooms to the archway that led into the vaults. I passed down a long and winding staircase, requesting him to be cautious as he followed. We came at length to the foot of the descent, and stood together on the damp ground of the catacombs of the Montresors.

The gait of my friend was unsteady, and the bells upon his cap jingled as he strode.

"The pipe?" said he.

"It is farther on," said I; "but observe the white web-work which gleams from these cavern walls."

He turned toward me, and looked into my eyes with two filmy orbs that distilled the rheum of intoxication.

"Nitre?" he asked, at length.

"Nitre," I replied. "How long have you had that cough?"

"Ugh! ugh! ugh!—ugh! ugh! ugh!—ugh! ugh! ugh!—ugh! ugh! ugh!—ugh! ugh! ugh!"

My poor friend found it impossible to reply for many minutes.

"It is nothing," he said, at last.

Roquelaire: A cloak.

"Come," I said, with decision, "we will go back; your health is precious. You are rich, respected, admired, beloved; you are happy, as once I was. You are a man to be missed. For me it is no matter. We will go back; you will be ill, and I cannot be responsible. Besides, there is Luchesi—"

"Enough," he said; "the cough is a mere nothing; it will not kill me. I shall not die of a cough."

"True—true," I replied; "and, indeed, I had no intention of alarming you unnecessarily; but you should use all proper caution. A draught of this Medoc will defend us from the damps."

Here I knocked off the neck of a bottle which I drew from a long row of its fellows that lay upon the mould.

"Drink," I said, presenting him the wine.

He raised it to his lips with a leer. He paused and nodded to me familiarly, while his bells jingled.

"I drink," he said, "to the buried that repose around us."

"And I to your long life."

He again took my arm, and we proceeded.

"These vaults," he said, "are extensive."

"The Montresors," I replied, "were a great and numerous family."

"I forget your arms."

"A huge human foot d'or,° in a field azure; the foot crushes a serpent rampant whose fangs are imbedded in the heel."

"And the motto?"

"Nemo me impune lacessit."°

"Good!" he said.

The wine sparkled in his eyes and the bells jingled. My own fancy grew warm with the Medoc. We had passed through walls of piled bones, with casks and puncheons intermingling into the inmost recesses of the catacombs. I paused again, and this time I made bold to seize Fortunato by an arm above the elbow.

"The nitre!" I said; "see, it increases. It hangs like moss upon the vaults. We are below the river's bed. The drops of moisture trickle among the bones. Come, we will go back ere it is too late. Your cough——"

"It is nothing," he said; "let us go on. But first, another draught of the Medoc."

I broke and reached him a flagon of De Grâve. He emptied it at a breath. His eyes flashed with a fierce light. He laughed and threw the bottle upward with a gesticulation I did not understand.

D'or: Of gold.
Nemo me impune lacessit: "No one wounds me with impunity"; the motto of the Scottish royal arms.

I looked at him in surprise. He repeated the movement—a grotesque one.

"You do not comprehend?" he said.

"Not I," I replied.

"Then you are not of the brotherhood."

"How?"

"You are not of the masons."

"Yes, yes," I said; "yes, yes."

"You? Impossible! A mason?"

"A mason," I replied.

"A sign," he said.

"It is this," I answered, producing a trowel from beneath the folds of my *roquelaire.*

"You jest," he exclaimed, recoiling a few paces. "But let us proceed to the Amontillado."

"Be it so," I said, replacing the tool beneath the cloak, and again offering him my arm. He leaned upon it heavily. We continued our route in search of the Amontillado. We passed through a range of low arches, descended, passed on, and descending again, arrived at a deep crypt, in which the foulness of the air caused our flambeaux rather to glow than flame.

At the most remote end of the crypt there appeared another less spacious. Its walls had been lined with human remains, piled to the vault overhead, in the fashion of the great catacombs of Paris. Three sides of this interior crypt were still ornamented in this manner. From the fourth the bones had been thrown down, and lay promiscuously upon the earth, forming at one point a mound of some size. Within the wall thus exposed by the displacing of the bones, we perceived a still interior recess, in depth about four feet, in width three, in height six or seven. It seemed to have been constructed for no especial use within itself, but formed merely the interval between two of the colossal supports of the roof of the catacombs, and was backed by one of their circumscribing walls of solid granite.

It was in vain that Fortunato, uplifting his dull torch, endeavored to pry into the depth of the recess. Its termination the feeble light did not enable us to see.

"Proceed," I said; "herein is the Amontillado. As for Luchesi——"

"He is an ignoramus," interrupted my friend, as he stepped unsteadily forward, while I followed immediately at his heels. In an instant he had reached the extremity of the niche, and finding his progress arrested by the rock, stood stupidly bewildered. A moment more and I had fettered him to the granite. In its surface were two iron staples, distant from each other about two feet, horizontally. From one of these depended a short chain, from the other a padlock. Throwing the links about his waist, it was but the work of a few seconds to secure it. He was too much astounded to resist. Withdrawing the key I stepped back from the recess. "Pass your hand," I said, "over the wall; you cannot help feeling the nitre. Indeed it is *very* damp. Once more let me *implore* you to return. No? Then I must positively leave you. But I must first render you all the little attentions in my power."

"The Amontillado!" ejaculated my friend, not yet recovered from his astonishment.

"True," I replied; "the Amontillado."

As I said these words I busied myself among the pile of bones of which I have before spoken. Throwing them aside, I soon uncovered a quantity of building stone and mortar. With these materials and with the aid of my trowel, I began vigorously to wall up the entrance of the niche.

I had scarcely laid the first tier of the masonry when I discovered that the intoxication of Fortunato had in a great measure worn off. The earliest indication I had of this was a low moaning cry from the depth of the recess. It was *not* the cry of a drunken man. There was then a long and obstinate silence. I laid the second tier, and the third, and the fourth; and then I heard the furious vibrations of the chain. The noise lasted for several minutes, during which, that I might hearken to it with the more satisfaction, I ceased my labors and sat down upon the bones. When at last the clanking subsided, I resumed the trowel, and finished without interruption the fifth, the sixth, and the seventh tier. The wall was now nearly upon a level with my breast. I again paused, and holding the flambeaux over the masonwork, threw a few feeble rays upon the figure within.

A succession of loud and shrill screams, bursting suddenly from the throat of the chained form, seemed to thrust me violently back. For a brief moment I hesitated—I trembled. Unsheathing my rapier, I began to grope with it about the recess; but the thought of an instant reassured me. I placed my hand upon the solid fabric of the catacombs, and felt satisfied. I reapproached the wall. I replied to the yells of him who clamored. I reechoed—I aided—I surpassed them in volume and in strength. I did this, and the clamorer grew still.

It was now midnight, and my task was drawing to a close. I had completed the eighth, the ninth, and the tenth tier. I had finished a portion of the last and the eleventh; there remained but a single stone to be fitted and plastered in. I struggled with its weight; I placed it partially in its destined position. But now there came from out the niche a low laugh that erected the hairs upon my head. It was succeeded by a sad voice, which·I had difficulty in recognizing as that of the noble Fortunato. The voice said—

"Ha! ha! ha!—he! he!—a very good joke indeed—an excellent jest.

We will have many a rich laugh about it at the palazzo—he! he! he!—over our wine—he! he! he!"

"The Amontillado!" I said.

"He! he! he!—he! he! he!—yes, the Amontillado. But is it not getting late? Will not they be awaiting us at the palazzo, the Lady Fortunato and the rest? Let us be gone."

"Yes," I said, "let us be gone."

"For the love of God, Montresor!"

"Yes," I said, "for the love of God!"

But to these words I hearkened in vain for a reply. I grew impatient. I called aloud:

"Fortunato!"

No answer. I called again:

"Fortunato!"

No answer still, I thrust a torch through the remaining aperture and let it fall within. There came forth in return only a jingling of the bells. My heart grew sick—on account of the dampness of the catacombs. I hastened to make an end of my labor. I forced the last stone into its position; I plastered it up. Against the new masonry I re-erected the old rampart of bones. For the half of a century no mortal has disturbed them. *In pace requiescat!*°

[1846]

In pace requiescat: May he rest in peace (Latin).

ROALD DAHL [1916–1990]

Lamb to the Slaughter

Born in Llandaff, Wales, **Roald Dahl** began working right out of high school, and at twenty-three, when World War II broke out, joined up with the Royal Air Force in Nairobi. After a fortuitous meeting with C.S. Forester in Washington, D.C., Dahl wrote an article for the *Saturday Evening Post* about his experiences in the war, thus launching his writing career. Originally published in the *New Yorker*, *Harper's*, and the *Atlantic Monthly*, his first stories were collected in *Over to You: Ten Stories of Flyers and Flying* (1946). Although he authored numerous other short-story collections, two novels, and several autobiographies, Dahl is most famous for children's literature, including *James and the Giant Peach* (1961) and *Charlie and the Chocolate Factory* (1964). A three-time winner of the Edgar Award from the Mystery Writers of America, Dahl died of a rare blood disorder at the age of seventy-four.

His best-known short story, "Lamb to the Slaughter," opens with Mary Maloney, the blissfully pregnant wife of police inspector Patrick Maloney, waiting for him to return home from a long day. Unexpectedly, Patrick tells Mary that he is leaving her. Mary kills him with a frozen leg of lamb, roasts it, and feeds it to the investigating police.

The room was warm and clean, the curtains drawn, the two table lamps alight—hers and the one by the empty chair opposite. On the sideboard behind her, two tall glasses, soda water, whiskey. Fresh ice cubes in the Thermos bucket.

Mary Maloney was waiting for her husband to come home from work.

Now and again she would glance up at the clock, but without anxiety, merely to please herself with the thought that each minute gone by made it nearer the time when he would come. There was a slow smiling air about her, and about everything she did. The drop of the head as she bent over her sewing was curiously tranquil. Her skin—for this was her sixth month with child—had acquired a wonderful translucent quality, the mouth was soft, and the eyes, with their new placid look, seemed larger, darker than before.

From *The Best of Roald Dahl*. Copyright renewed 1973, 1976, 1977 by Roald Dahl. A Vintage Original, 1978, published by Random House, Inc.

144

When the clock said ten minutes to five, she began to listen, and a few moments later, punctually as always, she heard the tires on the gravel outside, and the car door slamming, the footsteps passing the window, the key turning in the lock. She laid aside her sewing, stood up, and went forward to kiss him as he came in.

"Hullo darling," she said.　　　　　　　　　　　　　　　　　　　　　　5

"Hullo," he answered.

She took his coat and hung it in the closet. Then she walked over and made the drinks, a strongish one for him, a weak one for herself; and soon she was back again in her chair with the sewing, and he in the other, opposite, holding the tall glass with both his hands, rocking it so the ice cubes tinkled against the side.

For her, this was always a blissful time of day. She knew he didn't want to speak much until the first drink was finished, and she, on her side, was content to sit quietly, enjoying his company after the long hours alone in the house. She loved to luxuriate in the presence of this man, and to feel—almost as a sunbather feels the sun—that warm male glow that came out of him to her when they were alone together. She loved him for the way he sat loosely in a chair, for the way he came in a door, or moved slowly across the room with long strides. She loved the intent, far look in his eyes when they rested on her, the funny shape of the mouth, and especially the way he remained silent about his tiredness, sitting still with himself until the whiskey had taken some of it away.

"Tired darling?"

"Yes," he said. "I'm tired." And as he spoke, he did an unusual thing.　10 He lifted his glass and drained it in one swallow although there was still half of it, at least half of it left. She wasn't really watching him, but she knew what he had done because she heard the ice cubes falling back against the bottom of the empty glass when he lowered his arm. He paused a moment, leaning forward in the chair, then he got up and went slowly over to fetch himself another.

"I'll get it!" she cried, jumping up.

"Sit down," he said.

When he came back, she noticed that the new drink was dark amber with the quantity of whiskey in it.

"Darling, shall I get your slippers?"

"No."　　　　　　　　　　　　　　　　　　　　　　　　　　　　　　15

She watched him as he began to sip the dark yellow drink, and she could see little oily swirls in the liquid because it was so strong.

"I think it's a shame," she said, "that when a policeman gets to be as senior as you, they keep him walking about on his feet all day long."

He didn't answer, so she bent her head again and went on with her sewing; but each time he lifted the drink to his lips, she heard the ice cubes clinking against the side of the glass.

"Darling," she said. "Would you like me to get you some cheese? I haven't made any supper because it's Thursday."

"No," he said.   20

"If you're too tired to eat out," she went on, "it's still not too late. There's plenty of meat and stuff in the freezer, and you can have it right here and not even move out of the chair."

Her eyes waited on him for an answer, a smile, a little nod, but he made no sign.

"Anyway," she went on, "I'll get you some cheese and crackers first."

"I don't want it," he said.

She moved uneasily in her chair, the large eyes still watching his face.   25 "But you *must* have supper. I can easily do it here. I'd like to do it. We can have lamb chops. Or pork. Anything you want. Everything's in the freezer."

"Forget it," he said.

"But darling, you *must* eat! I'll fix it anyway, and then you can have it or not, as you like."

She stood up and placed her sewing on the table by the lamp.

"Sit down," he said. "Just for a minute, sit down."

It wasn't till then that she began to get frightened.   30

"Go on," he said. "Sit down."

She lowered herself back slowly into the chair, watching him all the time with those large, bewildered eyes. He had finished the second drink and was staring down into the glass, frowning.

"Listen," he said. "I've got something to tell you."

"What is it, darling? What's the matter?"

He had now become absolutely motionless, and he kept his head down   35 so that the light from the lamp beside him fell across the upper part of his face, leaving the chin and mouth in shadow. She noticed there was a little muscle moving near the corner of his left eye.

"This is going to be a bit of a shock to you, I'm afraid," he said. "But I've thought about it a good deal and I've decided the only thing to do is tell you right away. I hope you won't blame me too much."

And he told her. It didn't take long, four or five minutes at most, and she sat very still through it all, watching him with a kind of dazed horror as he went further and further away from her with each word.

"So there it is," he added. "And I know it's kind of a bad time to be telling you, but there simply wasn't any other way. Of course I'll give you money and see you're looked after. But there needn't really be any fuss. I hope not anyway. It wouldn't be very good for my job."

Her first instinct was not to believe any of it, to reject it all. It occurred

146

to her that perhaps he hadn't even spoken, that she herself had imagined the whole thing. Maybe, if she went about her business and acted as though she hadn't been listening, then later, when she sort of woke up again, she might find none of it had ever happened.

"I'll get the supper," she managed to whisper, and this time he didn't 40 stop her.

When she walked across the room she couldn't feel her feet touching the floor. She couldn't feel anything at all—except a slight nausea and a desire to vomit. Everything was automatic now—down the steps to the cellar, the light switch, the deep freeze, the hand inside the cabinet taking hold of the first object it met. She lifted it out, and looked at it. It was wrapped in paper, so she took off the paper and looked at it again.

A leg of lamb.

All right then, they would have lamb for supper. She carried it upstairs, holding the thin bone-end of it with both her hands, and as she went through the living-room, she saw him standing over by the window with his back to her, and she stopped.

"For God's sake," he said, hearing her, but not turning round. "Don't make supper for me. I'm going out."

At that point, Mary Maloney simply walked up behind him and with- 45 out any pause she swung the big frozen leg of lamb high in the air and brought it down as hard as she could on the back of his head.

She might just as well have hit him with a steel club.

She stepped back a pace, waiting, and the funny thing was that he remained standing there for at least four or five seconds, gently swaying. Then he crashed to the carpet.

The violence of the crash, the noise, the small table overturning, helped bring her out of the shock. She came out slowly, feeling cold and surprised, and she stood for a while blinking at the body, still holding the ridiculous piece of meat tight with both hands.

All right, she told herself. So I've killed him.

It was extraordinary, now, how clear her mind became all of a sudden. 50 She began thinking very fast. As the wife of a detective, she knew quite well what the penalty would be. That was fine. It made no difference to her. In fact, it would be a relief. On the other hand, what about the child? What were the laws about murderers with unborn children? Did they kill them both—mother and child? Or did they wait until the tenth month? What did they do?

Mary Maloney didn't know. And she certainly wasn't prepared to take a chance.

She carried the meat into the kitchen, placed it in a pan, turned the oven on high, and shoved it inside. Then she washed her hands and ran upstairs to the bedroom. She sat down before the mirror, tidied her hair, touched up her lips and face. She tried a smile. It came out rather peculiar. She tried again.

"Hullo Sam," she said brightly, aloud.

The voice sounded peculiar too.

"I want some potatoes please, Sam. Yes, and I think a can of peas." 55
That was better. Both the smile and the voice were coming out better now. She rehearsed it several times more. Then she ran downstairs, took her coat, went out the back door, down the garden, into the street.

It wasn't six o'clock yet and the lights were still on in the grocery shop. "Hullo Sam," she said brightly, smiling at the man behind the counter.

"Why, good evening, Mrs. Maloney. How're *you*?"

"I want some potatoes please, Sam. Yes, and I think a can of peas." 60
The man turned and reached up behind him on the shelf for the peas.

"Patrick's decided he's tired and doesn't want to eat out tonight," she told him. "We usually go out Thursdays, you know, and now he's caught me without any vegetables in the house."

"Then how about meat, Mrs. Maloney?"

"No, I've got meat, thanks. I got a nice leg of lamb from the freezer."

"Oh." 65

"I don't much like cooking it frozen, Sam, but I'm taking a chance on it this time. You think it'll be all right?"

"Personally," the grocer said, "I don't believe it makes any difference. You want these Idaho potatoes?"

"Oh yes, that'll be fine. Two of those."

"Anything else?" The grocer cocked his head on one side, looking at her pleasantly. "How about afterwards? What you going to give him for afterwards?"

"Well—what would you suggest, Sam?" 70
The man glanced around his shop. "How about a nice big slice of cheesecake? I know he likes that."

"Perfect," she said. "He loves it."

And when it was all wrapped and she had paid, she put on her brightest smile and said, "Thank you, Sam. Goodnight."

"Goodnight, Mrs. Maloney. And thank *you*."

And now, she told herself as she hurried back, all she was doing now, 75
she was returning home to her husband and he was waiting for his supper; and she must cook it good, and make it as tasty as possible because the poor man was tired; and if, when she entered the house, she happened to find anything unusual, or tragic, or terrible, then naturally it would be a shock and she'd become frantic with grief and horror. Mind you, she wasn't *expecting* to find anything. She was just going home with the vegetables. Mrs. Patrick Maloney going home with the vegetables on Thursday evening to cook supper for her husband.

That's the way, she told herself. Do everything right and natural. Keep things absolutely natural and there'll be no need for any acting at all.

Therefore, when she entered the kitchen by the back door, she was humming a little tune to herself and smiling.

"Patrick!" she called. "How are you, darling?"

She put the parcel down on the table and went through into the living room; and when she saw him lying there on the floor with his legs doubled up and one arm twisted back underneath his body, it really was rather a shock. All the old love and longing for him welled up inside her, and she ran over to him, knelt down beside him, and began to cry her heart out. It was easy. No acting was necessary.

A few minutes later she got up and went to the phone. She knew the 80 number of the police station, and when the man at the other end answered, she cried to him, "Quick! Come quick! Patrick's dead!"

"Who's speaking?"

"Mrs. Maloney. Mrs. Patrick Maloney."

"You mean Patrick Maloney's dead?"

"I think so," she sobbed. "He's lying on the floor and I think he's dead."

"Be right over," the man said. 85

The car came very quickly, and when she opened the front door, two policemen walked in. She knew them both—she knew nearly all the men at that precinct—and she fell right into Jack Noonan's arms, weeping hysterically. He put her gently into a chair, then went over to join the other one, who was called O'Malley, kneeling by the body.

"Is he dead?" she cried.

"I'm afraid he is. What happened?"

Briefly, she told her story about going out to the grocer and coming back to find him on the floor. While she was talking, crying and talking, Noonan discovered a small patch of congealed blood on the dead man's head. He showed it to O'Malley who got up at once and hurried to the phone.

Soon, other men began to come into the house. First a doctor, then 90 two detectives, one of whom she knew by name. Later, a police photographer arrived and took pictures, and a man who knew about fingerprints. There was a great deal of whispering and muttering beside the corpse, and the detectives kept asking her a lot of questions. But they always treated her kindly. She told her story again, this time right from the beginning, when Patrick had come in, and she was sewing, and he was tired, so tired he hadn't wanted to go out for supper. She told how she'd put the meat in the oven—"it's there now, cooking"—and how she'd slipped out to the grocer for vegetables, and come back to find him lying on the floor.

"Which grocer?" one of the detectives asked.

149

She told him, and he turned and whispered something to the other detective who immediately went outside into the street.

In fifteen minutes he was back with a page of notes, and there was more whispering, and through her sobbing she heard a few of the whispered phrases—"...acted quite normal...very cheerful...wanted to give him a good supper...peas...cheesecake...impossible that she..."

After a while, the photographer and the doctor departed and two other men came in and took the corpse away on a stretcher. Then the fingerprint man went away. The two detectives remained, and so did the two policemen. They were exceptionally nice to her, and Jack Noonan asked if she wouldn't rather go somewhere else, to her sister's house perhaps, or to his own wife who would take care of her and put her up for the night.

No, she said. She didn't feel she could move even a yard at the moment. Would they mind awfully if she stayed just where she was until she felt better. She didn't feel too good at the moment, she really didn't.

Then hadn't she better lie down on the bed? Jack Noonan asked.

No, she said. She'd like to stay right where she was, in this chair. A little later perhaps, when she felt better, she would move.

So they left her there while they went about their business, searching the house. Occasionally one of the detectives asked her another question. Sometimes Jack Noonan spoke at her gently as he passed by. Her husband, he told her, had been killed by a blow on the back of the head administered with a heavy blunt instrument, almost certainly a large piece of metal. They were looking for the weapon. The murderer may have taken it with him, but on the other hand he may've thrown it away or hidden it somewhere on the premises.

"It's the old story," he said. "Get the weapon, and you've got the man."

Later, one of the detectives came up and sat beside her. Did she know, he asked, of anything in the house that could've been used as the weapon? Would she mind having a look around to see if anything was missing—a very big spanner, for example, or a heavy metal vase.

They didn't have any heavy metal vases, she said.

"Or a big spanner?"

She didn't think they had a big spanner. But there might be some things like that in the garage.

The search went on. She knew that there were other policemen in the garden all around the house. She could hear their footsteps on the gravel outside, and sometimes she saw the flash of a torch through a chink in the curtains. It began to get late, nearly nine she noticed by the clock on the mantle. The four men searching the rooms seemed to be growing weary, a trifle exasperated.

95

100

"Jack," she said, the next time Sergeant Noonan went by. "Would you 105
mind giving me a drink?"

"Sure I'll give you a drink. You mean this whiskey?"

"Yes please. But just a small one. It might make me feel better."

He handed her the glass.

"Why don't you have one yourself," she said. "You must be awfully
tired. Please do. You've been very good to me."

"Well," he answered. "It's not strictly allowed, but I might take just a 110
drop to keep me going."

One by one the others came in and were persuaded to take a little nip
of whiskey. They stood around rather awkwardly with the drinks in their
hands, uncomfortable in her presence, trying to say consoling things to
her. Sergeant Noonan wandered into the kitchen, came out quickly and
said, "Look, Mrs. Maloney. You know that oven of yours is still on, and
the meat still inside."

"Oh *dear* me!" she cried. "So it is!"

"I better turn it off for you, hadn't I?"

"Will you do that, Jack? Thank you so much."

When the sergeant returned the second time, she looked at him with 115
her large, dark, tearful eyes. "Jack Noonan," she said.

"Yes?"

"Would you do me a small favour—you and these others?"

"We can try, Mrs. Maloney."

"Well," she said. "Here you all are, and good friends of dear Patrick's
too, and helping to catch the man who killed him. You must be terribly
hungry by now because it's long past your suppertime, and I know
Patrick would never forgive me, God bless his soul, if I allowed you to
remain in his house without offering you decent hospitality. Why don't
you eat up that lamb that's in the oven. It'll be cooked just right by now."

"Wouldn't dream of it," Sergeant Noonan said. 120

"Please," she begged. "Please eat it. Personally I couldn't touch a thing,
certainly not what's been in the house when he was here. But it's all right
for you. It'd be a favour to me if you'd eat it up. Then you can go on with
your work again afterwards."

There was a good deal of hesitating among the four policemen, but
they were clearly hungry, and in the end they were persuaded to go into
the kitchen and help themselves. The woman stayed where she was, listening to them through the open door, and she could hear them speaking
among themselves, their voices thick and sloppy because their mouths
were full of meat.

"Have some more, Charlie?"

"No. Better not finish it."

"She *wants* us to finish it. She said so. Be doing her a favour." 125

151

"Okay then. Give me some more."

"That's a hell of a big club the guy must've used to hit poor Patrick," one of them was saying. "The doc says his skull was smashed all to pieces just like from a sledgehammer."

"That's why it ought to be easy to find."

"Exactly what I say."

"Whoever done it, they're not going to be carrying a thing like that 130 around with them longer than they need."

One of them belched.

"Personally, I think it's right here on the premises."

"Probably right under our very noses. What you think, Jack?"

And in the other room, Mary Maloney began to giggle.

GUY DE MAUPASSANT [1850-1893]

Mother Savage

Guy de Maupassant did not consider a literary career until he was almost thirty years of age. After military service he worked as a French government clerk until 1882. Elements of the Franco-Prussian War of 1870 are part of several of his stories. This humiliating military defeat for France also provides the background for "Mother Savage." Maupassant's focus on the unglamorous realities of both rural and urban life mark him as one of the masters of literary naturalism, and his careful plot construction and attention to detail set high standards for later writers of short fiction. This story was translated by Lafcadio Hern.

Fifteen years had passed since I was at Virelogne. I returned there in the autumn to shoot with my friend Serval, who had at last rebuilt his chateau, which the Prussians had destroyed.

I loved that district. It is one of those delightful spots which have a sensuous charm for the eyes. You love it with a physical love. We, whom the country enchants, keep tender memories of certain springs, certain woods, certain pools, certain hills seen very often which have stirred us like joyful events. Sometimes our thoughts turn back to a corner in a forest, or the end of a bank, or an orchard filled with flowers, seen but a single time on some bright day, yet remaining in our hearts like the image of certain women met in the street on a spring morning in their light, gauzy dresses, leaving in soul and body an unsatisfied desire which is not to be forgotten, a feeling that you have just passed by happiness.

At Virelogne I loved the whole countryside, dotted with little woods and crossed by brooks which sparkled in the sun and looked like veins carrying blood to the earth. You fished in them for crawfish, trout and eels. Divine happiness! You could bathe in places and you often found snipe among the high grass which grew along the borders of these small water courses.

I was stepping along light as a goat, watching my two dogs running ahead of me, Serval, a hundred meters to my right, was beating a field of lucerne. I turned round by the thicket which forms the boundary of the wood of Sandres and I saw a cottage in ruins.

Suddenly I remembered it as I had seen it the last time, in 1869, neat, covered with vines, with chickens before the door. What is sadder than a dead house, with its skeleton standing bare and sinister?

I also recalled that inside its doors, after a very tiring day, the good woman had given me a glass of wine to drink and that Serval had told me the history of its people. The father, an old poacher, had been killed by the gendarmes. The son, whom I had once seen, was a tall, dry fellow who also passed for a fierce slayer of game. People called them *Les Sauvage.*

Was that a name or a nickname?

I called to Serval. He came up with his long strides like a crane.

I asked him, "What's become of those people?"

This was his story:

When war was declared the son Savage, who was then thirty-three years old, enlisted, leaving his mother alone in the house. People did not pity the old woman very much because she had money; they knew it.

She remained entirely alone in that isolated dwelling, so far from the village, on the edge of the wood. She was not afraid, however, being of the same strain as the men folk—a hardy old woman, tall and thin, who seldom laughed and with whom one never jested. The women of the fields laugh but little in any case, that is men's business. But they themselves have sad and narrowed hearts, leading a melancholy, gloomy life. The peasants imbibe a little noisy merriment at the tavern, but their helpmates always have grave, stern countenances. The muscles of their faces have never learned the motions of laughter.

Mother Savage continued her ordinary existence in her cottage, which was soon covered by the snows. She came to the village once a week to get bread and a little meat. Then she returned to her house. As there was talk of wolves, she went out with a gun upon her shoulder—her son's gun, rusty and with the butt worn by the rubbing of the hand—and she was a strange sight, the tall Savage, a little bent, going with slow strides over the snow, the muzzle of the piece extending beyond the black headdress, which confined her head and imprisoned her white hair, which no one had ever seen.

One day a Prussian force arrived. It was billeted upon the inhabitants, according to the property and resources of each. Four were allotted to the old woman, who was known to be rich.

They were four great fellows with fair complexion, blond beards and blue eyes, who had not grown thin in spite of the fatigue which they had endured already and who also, though in a conquered country, had remained kind and gentle. Alone with this aged woman, they showed themselves full of consideration, sparing her, as much as they could, all expense and fatigue. They could be seen, all four of them, making their toilet at the well in their shirt-sleeves in the gray dawn, splashing with great swishes of water their pink-white northern skin, while *La Mère Sauvage* went and came, preparing their soup. They would be seen cleaning the kitchen, rubbing the tiles, splitting wood, peeling potatoes, doing up all the housework like four good sons around their mother.

But the old woman thought always of her own son, so tall and thin, with his hooked nose and his brown eyes and his heavy mustache which made a roll of black hair upon his lip. She asked every day of each of the soldiers who were installed beside her hearth, "Do you know where the French marching regiment, No. 23, was sent? My boy is in it."

They invariably answered, "No, we don't know, don't know a thing at all." And, understanding her pain and her uneasiness—they who had mothers, too, there at home—they rendered her a thousand little services. She loved them well, moreover, her four enemies, since the peasantry have no patriotic hatred; that belongs to the upper class alone. The humble, those who pay the most because they are poor and because every new burden crushes them down; those who are killed in masses, who make the true cannon's prey because they are so many; those, in fine, who suffer most cruelly the atrocious miseries of war because they are the feeblest and offer least resistance—they hardly understand at all those bellicose ardors, that excitable sense of honor or those pretended political combinations which in six months exhaust two nations, the conqueror with the conquered.

They said in the district, in speaking of the Germans of Mother Savage, "There are four who have found a soft place."

Now, one morning, when the old woman was alone in the house, she observed, far off on the plain, a man coming toward her dwelling. Soon she recognized him; it was the postman to distribute the letters. He gave her a folded paper and she drew out of her case the spectacles which she used for sewing. Then she read:

MADAME SAUVAGE: This letter is to tell you sad news. Your boy Victor was killed yesterday by a shell which almost cut him in two. I was near by, as we stood next each other in the company, and he told me about you and asked me to let you know on the same day if anything happened to him.

I took his watch, which was in his pocket, to bring it back to you when the war is done.

CESAIRE RIVOT, Soldier of the 2d class, March. Reg. No. 23.

The letter was dated three weeks back.

She did not cry at all. She remained motionless, so overcome and stupefied that she did not even suffer as yet. She thought, "There's Victor killed now." Then little by little the tears came to her eyes and the sorrow filled her heart. Her thoughts came, one by one, dreadful, torturing. She would never kiss him again, her child, her big boy, never again! The gendarmes had killed the father; the Prussians had killed the son. He had been cut in two by a cannon-ball. She seemed to see the thing, the horrible thing: the head falling, the eyes open, while he chewed the corner of his big mustache as he always did in moments of anger.

What had they done with his body afterward? If they had only let her have her boy back as they had brought back her husband—with the bullet in the middle of the forehead!

But she heard a noise of voices. It was the Prussians returning from the village. She hid her letter very quickly in her pocket, and she received them quietly, with her ordinary face, having had time to wipe her eyes.

They were laughing, all four, delighted, for they brought with them a fine rabbit—stolen, doubtless—and they made signs to the old woman that there was to be something good to east.

She set herself to work at once to prepare breakfast, but when it came to killing the rabbit, her heart failed her. And yet it was not the first. One of the soldiers struck it down with a blow of his fist behind the ears.

The beast once dead, she skinned the red body, but the sight of the blood which she was touching, and which covered her hands, and which she felt cooling and coagulating, made her tremble from head to foot, and she kept seeing her big boy cut in two, bloody, like this still palpitating animal.

She sat down at table with the Prussians, but she could not eat, not even a mouthful. They devoured the rabbit without bothering themselves about her. She looked at them sideways, without speaking, her face so impassive that they perceived nothing.

All of a sudden she said, "I don't even know your names, and here's a whole month that we've been together." They understood, not without difficulty, what she wanted, and told their names.

That was not sufficient; she had them written for her on a paper, with the addresses of their families, and, resting her spectacles on her great nose, she contemplated that strange handwriting, then folded the sheet and put it in her pocket, on top of the letter which told her of the death of her son.

When the meal was ended she said to the men, "I am going to work for you."·

And she began to carry up hay into the loft where they slept.

They were astonished at her taking all this trouble; she explained to them that thus they would not be so cold; and they helped her. They heaped the stacks of hay as high as the straw roof, and in that manner they made a sort of great chamber with four walls of fodder, warm and perfumed, where they should sleep splendidly.

At dinner one of them was worried to see that Mother Savage still ate nothing. She told him that she had pains in her stomach. Then she kindled a good fire to warm herself, and the four Germans ascended to their lodging-place by the ladder which served them every night for this purpose.

As soon as they closed the trapdoor the old woman removed the ladder, then opened the outside door noiselessly and went back to look for more bundles of straw, with which she filled her kitchen.

She went barefoot in the snow, so softly that no sound was heard. From time to time she listened to the sonorous and unequal snoring of the four soldiers who were fast asleep.

When she judged her preparations to be sufficient, she threw one of the bundles into the fireplace, and when it was alight she scattered it over all the others. Then she went outside again and looked.

In a few seconds the whole interior of the cottage was illumined with a brilliant light and became a frightful brazier, a gigantic fiery furnace, whose glare streamed out of the narrow window and threw a glittering beam upon the snow.

Then a great cry issued from the top of the house; it was a clamor of men shouting heartrending calls of anguish and of terror. Finally the trapdoor having given way, a whirlwind of fire shot up into the loft, pierced the straw roof, rose to the sky like the immense flame of a torch, and all the cottage flared.

Nothing more was heard therein but the crackling of the fire, the cracking of the walls, the falling of the rafters. Suddenly the roof fell in and the burning carcass of the dwelling hurled a great plume of sparks into the air, amid a cloud of smoke.

The country, all white, lit up by the fire, shone like a cloth of silver tinted with red.

A bell, far off, began to toll.

The old "Savage" stood before her ruined dwelling, armed with her gun, her son's gun, for fear one of those men might escape.

When she saw that it was ended, she threw her weapon into the brasier. A loud report followed.

People were coming, the peasants, the Prussians.

They found the woman seated on the trunk of a tree, calm and satisfied.

A German officer, but speaking French like a son of France, demanded, "Where are your soldiers?"

She reached her bony arm toward the red heap of fire which was almost out and answered with a strong voice, "There!"

They crowded round her. The Prussian asked, "How did it take fire?"

"It was I who set it on fire."

They did not believe her, they thought that the sudden disaster had made her crazy. While all pressed round and listened, she told the story from beginning to end, from the arrival of the letter to the last shriek of the men who were burned with her house, and never omitted a detail.

When she had finished, she drew two pieces of paper from her pocket, and, in order to distinguish them by the last gleams of the fire, she again adjusted her spectacles. Then she said, showing one, "That, that is the death of Victor." Showing the other, she added, indicating the red ruins with a bend of the head, "Here are their names, so that you can write home." She quietly held a sheet of paper out to the officer, who held her by the shoulders, and she continued, "You must write how it happened, and you must say to their mothers that it was I who did that, Victoire Simon, the Savage! Do not forget."

The officer shouted some orders in German. They seized her, they threw her against the walls of her house, still hot. Then twelve men drew quickly up before her, at twenty paces. She did not move. She had understood; she waited.

An order rang out, followed instantly by a long report. A belated shot went off by itself, after the others.

The old woman did not fall. She sank as though they had cut off her legs.

The Prussian officer approached. She was almost cut in two, and in her withered hand she held her letter bathed with blood.

My friend Serval added, "It was by way of reprisal that the Germans destroyed the chateau of the district, which belonged to me."

I thought of the mothers of those four fine fellows burned in that house and of the horrible heroism of that other mother shot against the wall.

And I picked up a little stone, still blackened by the flames.

Lit. as Poetry

Writing about Poems

As with stories, there are certain elements you should be aware of as you prepare to write about poetry. Sometimes these elements are the same as for fiction. A **narrative poem**, for instance, will have a **plot**, **setting**, and **characters**, and all poems speak from a particular point of view. To the extent that any of the elements of fiction help you to understand a poem, by all means use them in your analysis. Poetry, however, does present a special set of concerns for a reader, and elements of poetry frequently provide rich ground for analysis.

ELEMENTS OF POETRY

The Speaker

First, consider the speaker of the poem. Imagine that someone is saying the words of this poem aloud. Who is speaking, where is this **speaker**, and what is his or her state of mind? Sometimes the voice is that of the poet him- or herself, but frequently a poem speaks from a different perspective, just as a short story might be from a point of view very different from the author's. It's not always apparent when this is the case, but some poets will signal who the speaker is in a title, as Christopher Marlowe does in "The Passionate Shepherd to His Love" or T. S. Eliot in "The Love Song of J. Alfred Prufrock." Be alert to signals that will help you recognize the speaker, and remember that some poems have more than one speaker.

The Listener

Be attentive also to any other persons in the poem, particularly an **implied listener**. Is there a "you" to whom the poem is addressed? If the poem is being spoken aloud, who is supposed to hear it? When, early in his poem "Dover Beach," Matthew Arnold writes, "Come to the window, sweet is the night-air!" he gives us an important clue as to how to read the poem. We should imagine both the speaker and the implied listener together in a room, with a window open to the night. As we read on, we

Janet E. Gardner, "Writing about Poems," from *Writing about Literature: A Portable Guide*, Second Edition with 2009 MLA Update, pages 82–91. Copyright © 2009 by Bedford/St. Martin's.

can look for further clues as to who these two people are and why they are together on this night. Many poems create a relationship between the "I" of the speaker and the "you" of the listener; however, that is not always the case. Sometimes the speaker does not address a "you" and instead provides a more philosophical meditation that isn't explicitly addressed to a listener. Consider the effect of these poems: Do they feel more abstract? More detached from the material conditions of time and place? Do they provide certainty, or resolution? The questions about the speaker and listener are crucial to your analysis of poetry.

Imagery

Just as you should be open to the idea that there are frequently symbols in stories, you should pay special attention to the **images** in poems. Although poems are often about such grand themes as love or death, they rarely dwell long in these abstractions. Rather, the best poetry seeks to make the abstraction concrete by creating vivid images appealing directly to the senses. A well-written poem will provide the mind of an attentive reader with sights, sounds, tastes, scents, and sensations. Since poems tend to be short and densely packed with meaning, every word and image is there for a reason. Isolate these images and give some thought to what they make you think and how they make you feel. Are they typical or unexpected?

Consider these lines from John Donne's "The Good Morrow":

> My face in thine eye, thine in mine appears,
> And true plain hearts do in the faces rest;
> Where can we find two better hemispheres,
> Without sharp north, without declining west? (lines 15–18)

Here, Donne celebrates the love between the speaker and his object of desire, comparing the faces of the lovers to two "hemispheres" on globes. Elsewhere in the poem, Donne uses imagery that is borrowed from the world of navigation and mapping; here, he suggests that the lovers' faces are an improvement upon whatever instruments explorers and learned men use to understand the world. By examining the images in a poem, their placement, juxtaposition, and effect, you will have gone a long way toward understanding the poem as a whole.

Sound and Sense

Of all the genres, poetry is the one that most self-consciously highlights **language**, so it is necessary to pay special attention to the sounds of a poem. In fact, it is always a good idea to read a poem aloud several times, giving yourself the opportunity to experience the role that sound plays in the poem's meaning.

Patterns of Sound

Much of the poetry written in English before the twentieth century was written in some form of **rhyme**, and contemporary poets continue to experiment with its effects. Rhymes may seem stilted or old-fashioned to our twenty-first-century ears, but keep in mind that rhymes have powerful social meanings in the cultural context in which they're written.

End-Rhymes

Here is just one example of an **end-rhyme** (rhymes that appear at the ends of lines in a poem). Let's look at a **heroic couplet** from Robert Browning's "My Last Duchess":

> Sir, 'twas all one! My favor at her breast,
> The dropping of the daylight in the West, (lines 25-26)

Here, Browning rhymes "breast" with "West," and in doing so equates them as part of a comparison. As you read poems, ask yourself how pairs of rhymes work. Do they create **juxtapositions**? Alignments of meaning? And what is the effect of that relationship as the poem progresses?

Assonance and Consonance

While it is important to look at the end of a line to see how the poet uses sounds, it is also important to look inside the line. Poets use **assonance** to create an aural effect among vowel sounds. Consider these opening lines from Gerard Manley Hopkins's "Pied Beauty":

> Glory be to God for dappled things —
>   For skies of couple-colour as a brinded cow;
>   For rose-moles all in stipple upon trout that swim;
> Fresh-firecoal chestnut-falls; finches' wings;
>   Landscape plotted and pieced — fold, fallow, and plough;
>   And all trades, their gear and tackle and trim. (lines 1-6)

Throughout these lines, Hopkins pays special attention to "uh" and "ow" sounds. Notice "couple-colour" and "cow" in line 2, "upon" and "trout" in line 3, "fallow" and "plough" in line 5. As you read through each line, ask yourself: Why does the poet align these sounds? Do these sounds speed up the tempo of the line, or slow it down? What do these sounds — and words — reveal about the poet's praise of "dappled things"?

Poets also use **consonance** to create alignments and juxtapositions among consonants. Consider these first lines from Christopher Marlowe's "The Passionate Shepherd to His Love":

> Come live with me and be my love,
>
> And we will all the pleasures prove (lines 1-2)

In line 1, Marlowe aligns "live" with "love" to suggest that there is an equation between cohabitation and romance. In line 2, he aligns the "p" sound in "pleasures prove"; in addition, though, the **slant rhyme** of "love" and "prove" also creates meaning between the lines. What "proof" is there in love? Is love what will make the speaker feel most alive?

Form

Poets writing in English use dozens of traditional forms from a variety of traditions. Some of the most common of these forms are the **sonnet**, the **villanelle**, the **sestina**, and the **ballad**, but there are too many to name here. As you read a poem in a traditional form, think of the form as a kind of template in which poets arrange and explore challenging emotional and intellectual material. A sonnet, for example, has a concise fourteen-line iambic pentameter structure that allows the poet to address a religious, romantic, or philosophical argument in a very compressed space. As you read a sonnet, you might ask yourself: What does its form accomplish that's different from, say, a ballad or **pantoum** or **triolet**?

Note, too, that many contemporary poets write in **free verse**, which means that they do not necessarily use a strict traditional form or meter for their poems. That doesn't mean that the free verse poet is writing without rules; it just means that the poet is creating his or her own system for the unique needs of each poem.

Meter

Poetry written in English is both **accentual** and **syllabic**. That is, poets count the number of accents as well as the number of syllables as they create each line of poetry. The most common meter in English poetry is **iambic pentameter**, which consists of five **accents** with two **syllables** in each accent. Consider the first four lines of John Donne's Holy Sonnet XIV ("Batter my heart"). Donne's lines are written in iambic pentameter, but have a lot of variation, too. As you read, notice where Donne places the emphasis in each line:

> **Bat**ter my **heart**, three-**per**soned God, for **you**
> As **yet** but **knock**, **breathe**, **shine**, and **seek** to **mend**;
> That **I** may **rise** and **stand**, o'er**throw** me, and **bend**
> Your **force** to **break**, **blow**, **burn**, and **make** me **new**. (lines 1–4)

Note that not every line is a perfect iamb; in line 1, Donne starts with an accent on the first syllable instead of the second one, disrupting the unstressed/stressed beat of the iambic line. Then, in line 2, Donne uses three strong monosyllabic words in a row to mimic the kind of aggression that the speaker requests from God. Donne does this again in line 4, with "break, blow, burn," which mirrors the sounds and sense of line 2. Donne continually disrupts the flow of iambic pentameter in order to reveal the difficulty of his spiritual struggle.

Iambic pentameter is only one of many kinds of meter in English, and each meter has its own unique properties and effects. When you read a poem, listen to each line to find out how many accents and syllables it contains, then determine what that meter is and how the poet uses—and subverts—that formula as part of a strategy for the poem.

Stanzas

A **stanza** is any grouping of lines of poetry into a unit. The word *stanza* comes from the Italian for "room." As you read poetry, imagine each stanza as a room with its own correspondences and relationships, and consider how that stanza creates a singular effect. Sometimes a stanza can be one line long; sometimes the poet creates a block of lines with no stanza breaks. All of these choices create distinct effects for readers of poetry.

Lineation

Lineation—or how a poet uses the lines in the poem—is a crucial component of poetry. Sometimes poets use punctuation at the end of every line, but more often they mix end-stopped lines with enjambed lines. **Enjambment** occurs when the line is not end-stopped with a comma, dash, or period. Its meaning spills over onto the next line, creating the effect of acceleration and intensity. Poets also use **caesuras** in the middle of lines to create variety in the pattern of the line. A caesura is a deep pause created by a comma, colon, semicolon, dash, period, or white space. Consider the use of enjambment and caesura in this excerpt from Browning's "My Last Duchess":

Or blush, at least. She thanked men, — good! but thanked
Somehow — I know not how — as if she ranked
My gift of a nine-hundred-years-old name
With anybody's gift. Who'd stoop to blame
This sort of trifling? Even had you skill (lines 31–35)

Look at the way Browning breaks up the monotony of the iambic
pentameter in this excerpt. He uses enjambment at the end of each line,
forcing the reader to move quickly through the line break to catch the
rest of the sentence's meaning in the following line. The long dashes
followed by "good!" and "I know not how" create a sense of remove
between what the speaker wants us to know versus what's going on
inside his head. Browning creates deep pauses, or caesuras, in lines 31
and 34 by ending one sentence and beginning a new one in the middle of
the line. With these variations, Browning enlivens his lines with cues for
a more dramatic performance of the poem.

There are many kinds of rhyme schemes, forms, and meters for poetry
written in English. For more information, see the "Elements of Poetry"
online tutorial at: http://bcs.bedfordstmartins.com/virtualit/poetry/rhyme_
def.html.

A POEM FOR ANALYSIS

Take a few minutes to read William Shakespeare's Sonnet 116 and consider the questions about it that follow. Although the poem is brief, it is
complex. What elements of poetry do you notice in it?

WILLIAM SHAKESPEARE   [1564–1616]

Sonnet 116

Let me not to the marriage of true minds
Admit impediments. Love is not love
Which alters when it alteration finds,
Or bends with the remover to remove.
O, no, it is an ever-fixèd mark   5
That looks on tempests and is never shaken;

It is the star to every wandering bark,°   *ship*
Whose worth's unknown, although his height be taken.°   *is measured*
Love's not time's fool, though rosy lips and cheeks
Within his bending sickle's compass come;   10
Love alters not with his brief hours and weeks,
But bears it out even to the edge of doom.°   *Judgment Day*
   If this be error and upon me proved,
   I never writ, nor no man ever loved.

[1609]

QUESTIONS ON THE POEM

☐ What **images** are most striking in this poem? Do they seem conventional, surprising, experimental? Why?

☐ A **sonnet** often reveals its own logic in order to argue for a point of view. What is the argument of this poem? Do you find it persuasive? If not, why not?

☐ What is the **rhyme** structure of this sonnet? What words are aligned as a result of this scheme?

☐ How does Shakespeare use **enjambment** and **caesura** to manage the tempo of the poem? What effects does this create?

SAMPLE PAPER: AN EXPLICATION

Patrick McCorkle, the author of the paper that follows, was given the assignment to perform a close reading of one of Shakespeare's sonnets. He needed first to pick a poem and then to choose specific features of its language to isolate and analyze. He chose Shakespeare's Sonnet 116 because it seemed to him to offer an interesting and balanced definition of love. After rereading the poem, he became interested in several unexpectedly negative, even unsettling images that seemed out of place in a poem about the positive emotion of love. This was a good start, and it allowed him to write a draft of the paper. When he was finished, however, the essay was a little shorter than he had hoped it would be. During a peer workshop in class, he discussed the sonnet and his draft with two classmates, and together they noticed how many negative words appeared in the poem as well. That was the insight Patrick needed to fill out his essay and feel satisfied with the results.

Patrick McCorkle
Professor Bobrick
English 102
10 January 2008

Shakespeare Defines Love

From the earliest written rhymes to the latest top-40 radio hit, love is among the eternal themes for poetry. Most love poetry seems to fall into one of two categories. Either the poet sings the praises of the beloved and the unending joys of love in overly exaggerated terms, or the poet laments the loss of love with such bitterness and distress that it seems like the end of life. Anyone who has been in love, though, can tell you that both of these views are limited and incomplete and that real love is neither entirely joyous nor entirely sad. In Sonnet 116, "Let me not to the marriage of true minds," Shakespeare creates a more realistic image of love. By balancing negative with positive images and language, this sonnet does a far better job than thousands of songs and poems before and since, defining love in all its complexities and contradictions.

Patrick identifies his topic and states his thesis.

Like many poems, Sonnet 116 relies on a series of visual images to paint vivid pictures for a reader, but not all of these images are what we might expect in a poem celebrating the pleasures of lasting love. A reader can easily picture "an ever-fixèd mark," a "tempest," a "star," a "wandering bark" (meaning a boat lost at sea), "rosy lips and cheeks," and a "bending sickle." Some of these, like stars and rosy lips, are just the sort of sunny, positive images we typically find in love poems of the joyous variety. Others, though, are more unexpected. Flowers and images of springtime, for instance, are standard issue in happy love poetry, but a sickle is associated with autumn and the death of the year, and metaphorically with death itself in the form of the grim reaper. Likewise, a boat tossed in a raging tempest is not exactly the typical poetic depiction of happy love.

Patrick introduces the poem's contradictory imagery.

Such pictures would hardly seem to provide an upbeat image of what love is all about, and in fact they might be more at home in one of the sad poems about the loss of love. But these tempests and sickles are more realistic than the hearts and flowers of so many lesser love poems. In fact, they show that the poet recognizes the bad times that occur in all relationships, even those strong enough to inspire love sonnets. And the negative images are tempered because of the contexts in which they occur. The "wandering bark" for instance might represent trouble and loss, but love itself is seen as the star that will lead the boat safely back to calm waters. Meanwhile, the beloved's "rosy lips and cheeks" may fade, but real love outlives even the stroke of death's sickle, lasting "to the edge of doom."

Patrick explains the effect of this imagery.

Just as positive and negative images are juxtaposed, so are positive and negative language. The first four lines of Sonnet 116 are made up of two sentences, both negatives, beginning with the words "Let me not" and "Love is not." The negatives of the first few lines continue in phrases like "Whose worth's unknown" and "Love's not time's fool." From here, the poem goes on to dwell in abstract ideas such as "alteration," "impediments," and "error." None of this is what readers of love poems have been led to expect in their previous reading, and we might even wonder if the poet finds this love thing worth the trouble. This strange and unexpected language continues on through the last line of the poem, which contains no fewer than three negative words: "never," "nor," and "no."

Patrick integrates direct quotations from the poem into his close reading.

Where, a reader might ask, are the expected positive descriptions of love? Where are the summer skies, the smiles and laughter? Clearly, Shakespeare doesn't mean to sweep his readers up in rosy images of a lover's bliss. Ultimately, though, even with the preponderance of negative images and words, the poem strikes a hopeful tone. The hedging about what love isn't and what it can't do are balanced with positive words and phrases, saying clearly what love is: "it is an ever-fixèd mark" and "it is the star." Love, it would seem, does not make our lives perfect, but it gives us the strength, stability, and direction to survive the bad times.

Though more than 400 years have passed since Shakespeare wrote his sonnets, some things never change, and among these is the nature of complex human emotions. In a mere fourteen lines, Shakespeare succeeds where many others have failed through the years, providing a much more satisfying definition of love than one normally sees in one-dimensional, strictly happy or sad poetry. The love he describes is the sort that not everyone is lucky enough to find — a "marriage of true minds" — complicated, unsettling, and very real.

In his conclusion, Patrick suggests that the poem is successful because of the juxtapositions he has discussed.

ROBERT FROST   [1874–1963]

Fire and Ice

Robert Frost (1874–1963) was born in San Francisco and lived there until he was eleven. When his father died, the family moved to Massachusetts, where Robert did well in school, especially in the classics, but later dropped out of both Dartmouth College and Harvard University. He went unrecognized as a poet until 1913, when he was first published in England, where he had moved with his wife and four children. Upon returning to the States, Frost quickly achieved success with more publications and became the most celebrated poet in mid-twentieth-century America. He held a teaching position at Amherst College and received many honorary degrees as well as an invitation to recite a poem at John F. Kennedy's inauguration. Although his work is principally associated with the life and landscape of New England, and although he was a poet of traditional verse forms and meters, he is also considered a quintessentially modern poet for his adherence to language as it is actually spoken, the psychological complexity of his portraits, and the degree to which his work is infused with layers of ambiguity and irony.

Some say the world will end in fire,
Some say in ice.
From what I've tasted of desire
I hold with those who favor fire.
But if it had to perish twice,
I think I know enough of hate
To say that for destruction ice
Is also great
And would suffice.

[1923]

Robert Frost, "Fire and Ice" from *The Poetry of Robert Frost*, edited by Edward Connery Lathem. Copyright © 1923, 1969 by Henry Holt and Company. Copyright © 1951 by Robert Frost. Reprinted by permission of Henry Holt and Company, LLC.

ROBERT FROST

Design

I found a dimpled spider, fat and white,
On a white heal-all, holding up a moth
Like a white piece of rigid satin cloth—
Assorted characters of death and blight
Mixed ready to begin the morning right,   5
Like the ingredients of a witches' broth—
A snow-drop spider, a flower like a froth,
And dead wings carried like a paper kite.

What had the flower to do with being white,
The wayside blue and innocent heal-all?   10
What brought the kindred spider to that height,
Then steered the white moth thither in the night?
What but design of darkness to appall?—
If design govern in a thing so small.

[1936]

Robert Frost, "Design" from *The Poetry of Robert Frost*, edited by Edward Connery
Lathem. Copyright © 1923, 1969 by Henry Holt and Company. Copyright © 1936,
1942, 1944, 1951 by Robert Frost. Copyright © 1964, 1970 by Lesley Frost
Ballantine. eprinted by permission of Henry Holt and Company, LLC.

ROBERT FROST

Stopping by Woods on a Snowy Evening

Whose woods these are I think I know.
His house is in the village, though;
He will not see me stopping here
To watch his woods fill up with snow.

My little horse must think it queer   5
To stop without a farmhouse near
Between the woods and frozen lake
The darkest evening of the year.

He gives his harness bells a shake
To ask if there is some mistake.   10
The only other sound's the sweep
Of easy wind and downy flake.

The woods are lovely, dark, and deep,
But I have promises to keep,
And miles to go before I sleep,   15
And miles to go before I sleep.

[1923]

"Stopping by Woods on a Snowy Evening" from *The Poetry of Robert Frost*, edited by Edward Connery Lathem. Copyright 1923, 1969 by Henry Holt and Co., and copyright 1951 by Robert Frost. Reprinted by permission of Henry Holt and Company, LLC.

ROBERT FROST

The Road Not Taken

Two roads diverged in a yellow wood,
And sorry I could not travel both
And be one traveler, long I stood
And looked down one as far as I could
To where it bent in the undergrowth;   5

Then took the other, as just as fair,
And having perhaps the better claim,
Because it was grassy and wanted wear;
Though as for that, the passing there
Had worn them really about the same,   10

And both that morning equally lay
In leaves no step had trodden black.
Oh, I kept the first for another day!
Yet knowing how way leads on to way,
I doubted if I should ever come back.   15

I shall be telling this with a sigh
Somewhere ages and ages hence:
Two roads diverged in a wood, and I—
I took the one less traveled by,
And that has made all the difference.   20

[1916]

ROBERT FROST

After Apple-Picking

My long two-pointed ladder's sticking through a tree
Toward heaven still,
And there's a barrel that I didn't fill
Beside it, and there may be two or three
Apples I didn't pick upon some bough.   5
But I am done with apple-picking now.
Essence of winter sleep is on the night,
The scent of apples: I am drowsing off.
I cannot rub the strangeness from my sight
I got from looking through a pane of glass   10
I skimmed this morning from the drinking trough
And held against the world of hoary grass.
It melted, and I let it fall and break.
But I was well
Upon my way to sleep before it fell,   15
And I could tell
What form my dreaming was about to take.
Magnified apples appear and disappear,
Stem end and blossom end,
And every fleck of russet showing clear.   20
My instep arch not only keeps the ache,
It keeps the pressure of a ladder-round.
I feel the ladder sway as the boughs bend.
And I keep hearing from the cellar bin
The rumbling sound   25
Of load on load of apples coming in.
For I have had too much
Of apple-picking: I am overtired
Of the great harvest I myself desired.
There were ten thousand thousand fruit to touch,   30
Cherish in hand, lift down, and not let fall.
For all
That struck the earth,
No matter if not bruised or spiked with stubble,
Went surely to the cider-apple heap   35
As of no worth.

One can see what will trouble
This sleep of mine, whatever sleep it is.
Were he not gone,
The woodchuck could say whether it's like his   40
Long sleep, as I describe its coming on,
Or just some human sleep.

[1914]

ROBERT FROST

Birches

When I see birches bend to left and right
Across the lines of straighter darker trees,
I like to think some boy's been swinging them.
But swinging doesn't bend them down to stay
As ice storms do. Often you must have seen them   5
Loaded with ice a sunny winter morning
After a rain. They click upon themselves
As the breeze rises, and turn many-colored
As the stir cracks and crazes their enamel.
Soon the sun's warmth makes them shed crystal shells   10
Shattering and avalanching on the snow crust—
Such heaps of broken glass to sweep away
You'd think the inner dome of heaven had fallen.
They are dragged to the withered bracken by the load,
And they seem not to break; though once they are bowed   15
So low for long, they never right themselves:
You may see their trunks arching in the woods
Years afterwards, trailing their leaves on the ground
Like girls on hands and knees that throw their hair
Before them over their heads to dry in the sun.   20
But I was going to say when Truth broke in
With all her matter of fact about the ice storm,
I should prefer to have some boy bend them
As he went out and in to fetch the cows—
Some boy too far from town to learn baseball,   25
Whose only play was what he found himself,
Summer or winter, and could play alone.
One by one he subdued his father's trees
By riding them down over and over again
Until he took the stiffness out of them,   30
And not one but hung limp, not one was left
For him to conquer. He learned all there was
To learn about not launching out too soon
And so not carrying the tree away
Clear to the ground. He always kept his poise   35
To the top branches, climbing carefully

With the same pains you use to fill a cup
Up to the brim, and even above the brim.
Then he flung outward, feet first, with a swish,
Kicking his way down through the air to the ground.   40
So was I once myself a swinger of birches.
And so I dream of going back to be.
It's when I'm weary of considerations,
And life is too much like a pathless wood
Where your face burns and tickles with the cobwebs   45
Broken across it, and one eye is weeping
From a twig's having lashed across it open.
I'd like to get away from earth awhile
And then come back to it and begin over.
May no fate willfully misunderstand me   50
And half grant what I wish and snatch me away
Not to return. Earth's the right place for love:
I don't know where it's likely to go better.
I'd like to go by climbing a birch tree,
And climb black branches up a snow-white trunk   55
Toward heaven, till the tree could bear no more,
But dipped its top and set me down again.
That would be good both going and coming back.
One could do worse than be a swinger of birches.

[1916]

177

ROBERT FROST

Mending Wall

Something there is that doesn't love a wall,
That sends the frozen-ground-swell under it,
And spills the upper boulders in the sun;
And makes gaps even two can pass abreast.
The work of hunters is another thing: 5
I have come after them and made repair
Where they have left not one stone on a stone,
But they would have the rabbit out of hiding,
To please the yelping dogs. The gaps I mean,
No one has seen them made or heard them made,   10
But at spring mending-time we find them there.
I let my neighbor know beyond the hill;
And on a day we meet to walk the line
And set the wall between us once again.
We keep the wall between us as we go.   15
To each the boulders that have fallen to each.
And some are loaves and some so nearly balls
We have to use a spell to make them balance:
"Stay where you are until our backs are turned!"
We wear our fingers rough with handling them.   20
Oh, just another kind of outdoor game,
One on a side. It comes to little more:
There where it is we do not need the wall:
He is all pine and I am apple orchard.
My apple trees will never get across   25
And eat the cones under his pines, I tell him.
He only says, "Good fences make good neighbors."
Spring is the mischief in me, and I wonder
If I could put a notion in his head:
"*Why* do they make good neighbors? Isn't it   30
Where there are cows? But here there are no cows.
Before I built a wall I'd ask to know
What I was walling in or walling out,
And to whom I was like to give offense.
Something there is that doesn't love a wall,   35
That wants it down." I could say "Elves" to him,

But it's not elves exactly, and I'd rather
He said it for himself. I see him there
Bringing a stone grasped firmly by the top
In each hand, like an old-stone savage armed.   40
He moves in darkness as it seems to me,
Not of woods only and the shade of trees.
He will not go behind his father's saying,
And he likes having thought of it so well
He says again, "Good fences make good neighbors."   45

[1914]